Awakening to *Peace, Love,* and *Happiness*

Alfredo Brandt

PAGE PUBLISHING, INC.
Conneaut Lake, PA

First originally published by Page Publishing 2021

ISBN 978-1-6624-3107-4 (pbk)
ISBN 978-1-6624-3192-0 (hc)
ISBN 978-1-6624-3108-1 (digital)

Printed in the United States of America

To my mom, dad, and brother, thank you
for always believing in my journey.
To all my friends and students, who helped
me find my truth in many ways.

Contents

Peace, Love, and Happiness

If you have felt like there has to be more to life, you should read this book. You are absolutely right: there is a whole lot more to life than your job title, your financial success, and your relationship status—and you are the only one holding yourself back. A little bit of peace, love, and happiness will serve all of us right now. That movement from the 1960s of breaking the patterns of society and just living with freedom can still apply to us today. There are no realities but just perspectives, and in this book I want to help change your perspective to see how much peace, love, and happiness you can have in your life. One thing in common with you and me is that we both have a calling inside, and we have the desire to answer the calling someday. Even though this might feel slightly far-fetched, the biggest obstacle you have to get out of the way is the way your mind is wired. Like any other relationship in your life, the success of the relationship is equivalent to how much understanding you have of the parties in it. Your life will always be a relationship with yourself, and you must understand who you are. Otherwise, it will continue to feel like life and its accomplishments are never enough. Countless numbers of self-help books and programs teach you all sorts of techniques to manifest abundance and take control of your life. But how can you manifest properly without understanding truly who you are and what you really want at your core? Are the things you say you want just programming from society, your parents, and the outside world? The teachings of this book will serve you to declutter your mind from all the labeling and collective thinking you have learned from the outside world. The goal is to wake you up and get you to know who you are, to make you proud of who you are, so you can finally start creating your freedom from a place of love.

I am not a radical, nor will I suggest that you grow hair out by the end of this book. I'm just one of the thousands of people who one day realized there had to be more to life than the hamster wheel I was trapped on for years. I kept chasing and checking accomplishments off my list, but I still wasn't feeling as great inside as I expected. Have you ever looked back at all the things you wanted in your life during your teenage years and compare it to what you want now as an adult? I had such a huge list. I wanted cars, houses, businesses, status, marriage, and looks—you name it. As the years have gone by and lessons have manifested in my life, I have simplified my wants into just feelings. I am now willing to do what it takes to bring freedom and peace into my life. That is awakening, realizing that nothing from the outside world will ever give you lasting happiness. The outside world will only patch your wounds. Same as when you patch a tire, it fixes the problem to help you get by for a while, but it will break again. That is what outside gains in your life have done and will continue to do for you. It will patch your life and give you temporary relief, but soon enough that relief fades.

Have you ever misplaced your keys and went searching for them, just to end up finding out that they were inside your pocket throughout your entire search? That is what awakening is all about: realizing that all we have searched for outside, we have carried with us all along throughout our lives. It's always called *awakening* and never *awakened*; we will forget over and over again where we place those keys. As used in this book, *awakening* is the term used to describe the moment you are no longer identified with your sense of self. When you start to see things for what they are, and not seeing yourself in them. It's the realization that our emotions and reactions do not depend on anything outside of us and we have full control over them. Awakening usually comes into our lives when we start questioning why we feel so tired, let down, and unhappy after so many years of hard work in all areas of our lives. Through self-observation, we gain enlightenment on how much of what we do is unnecessary if what we really want is to gain peace, love, and happiness. *Awakening*, if anything, will just remove clutter from your life and will peel back the layers and show that you are drained from overthinking, overdoing, and pretending too much. It is as simple as waking up to who you are.

Awakening is always happening; it is a daily habit. Awakening is something that, for most of us, will always be something to be worked for in this lifetime, and it is supported by daily habits that keep us awake. Understanding the concept of awakening simply isn't enough. You probably know that you should find yourself deserving of love; you probably know that you should be identifying and living your own life purpose. You have already heard thousands of times that you should be happy on your own. But how? How can I be happy when I feel incomplete for not being with my soul mate before the age of thirty? How can I live my purpose when I still must pay my bills? How can I engage in this life of putting myself first when I live in a world that demands constantly for me to put myself last? I am going to guess that most people understand at some level what they should be doing to fulfill their spiritual needs, but they fail to find a way to put it into practice within their present circumstances.

Many authors have attempted to answer life's biggest questions and have written some empowering pieces to get people motivated to create the life of their dreams. While I believe that most personal-growth authors have good intentions, the biggest missing piece is how do you start where you are? My journey in personal growth began with the release of the movie *The Secret*. I used to watch it almost daily because it truly made me feel so good about my future and where I was headed. It was an empowering masterpiece in getting people like myself motivated to find themselves deserving of all the things they wanted. After countless hours making vision boards, saying affirmations, and pretending to be a millionaire, I did not create too much of the abundance I was after. Was it user error? Maybe. At the time, I didn't have the belief system to understand what I was asking for, and that journey left me feeling like my life wasn't enough, but yet I still kept the positive mindset to try to become more.

Later on, I encountered the incredible teachings of Eckhart Tolle, for which I am so grateful. I felt like he came from a different perspective and helped me gain peace with who I was. I finally learned to be present in the moment and accept my life for what it is. Between *The Secret* and Eckhart's teachings, I was left in a paradox where anything I might desire was labeled to come from my ego, and yet accepting the present became living in a state of nonaction and giving up on life. This book is my path out of that paradox: we are deserving of more, and we have the power to create what we want. But we first must do our homework and become present to understand who we truly are. We must start practicing awakening and find freedom from the patterns of society. We must create the life we dream from a place of love and not fear. It is okay to want things in life; the missing piece is to remain awake, so our happiness never depends on those things.

What we keep missing all along is that our success as a society depends on people being their best, most authentic selves. People acting from a place of love, energized to do and help, and that can only come as light that shines from within us. Blind action is not enough. Doing for the sake of doing will not let our light shine. Instead, we need to create our life internally from a place of consciousness and awareness. The fire must be built internally first. When we feel this energy internally is when we have the power to manifest a life that we enjoy living in. If we keep operating outside of ourselves, all we do is recreate the same world repeatedly. We keep ignoring our true calling and, as a result, create more suffering for ourselves and others.

Why don't we intuitively know all of this information and live our best lives? It's simple. As children, we knew it, and as adults we have forgotten.

For example, I am considerably fast at typing on a keyboard. I have typed on keyboards for many years, so I do not have to look down anymore. I have never questioned how my fingers find the right keys, but they just do. A couple nights ago I had to type my e-mail using a TV remote control at home, and I was shocked at how hard it was for me to find the right letters. For a moment I even questioned the keyboard itself. Why can't I find the *b* and the *f?* Our minds are incredible machines. They memorize processes, so they can be efficient and reduce the amount of conscious energy spent on certain tasks. I guarantee you, at one point I could consciously tell you where each letter in the keyboard is at, but once I found a way to memorize it, I never had to remember it again.

This is the same thing that happened to your ability to be at peace, your ability to love yourself and to be happy. We memorized the keyboard the same way we memorized our daily routines. And we lost awareness of how to actually tap into our feelings. We know how to do things, but we can't remember why we do them. Go back to your childhood and remember the games you used to play. As kids, we could take a rock and imagine it was a car; we could see ourselves as any role we wanted to play. Our self-worth wasn't in question, and we didn't identify with any roles; we could just go back to our happy thoughts, our peaceful state, and our loving mind without any troubles. As years go by, more and more is demanded from us by the world. School, sports, activities, homework, and then the social pressures of your generation. The mind becomes so occupied now in a constant state of satisfying the outside world. We are now being forced to play roles like being a dad, a mom, a lawyer, a boss, a husband, a wife, and you memorize those roles just like you memorize your keyboard. The only thing you are rarely asked to do is to be you for who you are, and just like me trying to find the letters on the TV screen, you occasionally try to figure out how to be at peace, or happy, or even in love by just being you.

Years can go by until we get to this point of awareness and look inside and wonder: is this it? You keep checking accomplishments off your list, but the fulfillment inside is not there. We have to be doing something wrong. And this is when the awakening begins. When you begin to look inside and take responsibility for what you have been doing to hold your true desires back. I won't tell you it is an easy experience because it has taken me years, and I am still learning more about who I am each day. But I will tell you it is worth it. I have lost so much fear of life, and I have freed myself from so many worthless attachments. Your success in the awakening journey will always be related to how much truth you can handle about yourself. For some, it is too scary to see the wounds that are still open inside, and it is easier to do what we have done all these years, which is settle for less than what we deserve. But having courage is being afraid but doing it anyway.

My goal is to help you find joy where you are right now. I know you can be happy now with whatever is going on in your life. I want you to make peace with your circumstances. I want you to feel grounded and know that your future is not dependent on dollar signs or insane amounts of work and action. Your peaceful, loving, and happy future depends on the amount of consciousness you bring to this moment. I am a firm believer that you can have everything you want in this lifetime, but first you need to know what you truly want and find yourself deserving of it. Look inside: are you okay with what is happening in your life right now? Is there something you are resisting? If you are not at peace with your present, if you don't think you have enough, and you are exhausted from trying so hard to manifest more into your life, then this book is for you. This book is for both you and me and for everyone who needs a daily, weekly, monthly, or yearly reminder of the freedom that comes along with awakening into peace, love, and happiness every day.

Awakening to Peace

Peace is one of the most treasured feelings in this life. Peace is simply being okay. When you are at peace, everything is fine, and there is no resistance to the circumstances; you flow with ease. You have an awareness that you will be okay no matter what circumstance comes your way. When I think of peace, my mind immediately relates it to nature, to those places that have not been disrupted by humankind. These places just exist in all their beauty without regard to humans. Nature is peaceful because it flows with no resistance. Whether a pouring rain or a powerful wave crashing against the shore moving everything on its path, it is always working together, surrendered, with no emotion around the event. It just is. You see animals in sync with the environment, in sync with the circumstances, and in sync with life and death itself. Nature is one with life. And both you and I are also meant to be one with life.

Our ego has gotten in the way over time and blinded us. We grew up in a society that idolizes power. It idolizes money, success, and status, and we begin to compete with one another. It creates in us a need to win. We want to gain more and more in order to feed our egos. At the same time, we still want to feel worthy. Our minds also crave to be loved, accepted, happy, and overjoyed, and we think these feelings will come from outside circumstances. We are so focused on what is outside of us that it is no accident that we expect the outside world to make us feel special. The ego makes you believe that you can control the people around you and the outside world to obtain the validation that you seek. At this point, we are not one with life anymore; we are resisting who we are and trying to change the events we currently face, in order to be where we think we are supposed to be, in order to feel "okay."

Once we stop being one with life, the first thing to go is peace. The moment you are not at ease with your present, you are no longer at peace. You are missing something. You realize that there is something you want right now that you do not have. At times, you will manage to find ways to get what you want. Your unconscious actions could still manifest the love of someone you like, or the car or house you want. But this will get you farther away from peace because it will further perpetuate the illusion that you are in control. You fall into a trap of wanting more and more; the chase never ends. You keep making up a story in your head that in order to have peace, you need to get more than what you already have. Having will never get you to this place of peace.

The only thing that is left is to realize that what you long for is already within you. That maybe peace is always with you, waiting for you to wake up and come join. Peace is not something we gain when we have mastered life or retire from our job. Peace is available for all of us regardless of who we are at that moment. Peace is like the background piano music at the lobby of a hotel. The lobby could be empty or full of people screaming. The piano is always playing in the background, and you make the conscious decision to tune in to the sound of the piano or to the noise people are making.

Peace is a flat line. It does not have emotions attached to it. The beauty of being at peace is that you are welcomed anytime. If you are doing great, then great. If you are feeling down, it's okay. Peace is being at ease with your life. You observe what is happening; you do what you can to respond to it, but you detach from the judgment. You are one with the magic of life. You have an unwavering faith that, no matter what, all you can be is you; all you can do is what you can, and no matter what you will be in line with your highest good.

One time I saw a reality show, and a cow was dying from a disease that didn't allow her to get up on her feet. It caught my attention because she was still drinking from the bowl of water the farmers left for her, and she was eating what was around her. The other cows also walked around her, and the day seemed to go like any other day. The energy of the scene was sad to watch because I knew the cow was sick. But the cow herself seemed very peaceful. The cow was okay, almost as though she understood and accepted her disease. She observed her circumstances, and she did what she could, knowing that whatever the results of her healing could be, she was in line with her highest good. That's living at peace. Being one with life. Nonresistance to what is.

If you took that story and changed the characters for humans...oh boy. Person is dying, family is crying around him, the patient is suffering, sadness all around. A horror scene. Not one bit peaceful. Humans are still observers of the situation; they still do what they can, but they are not okay with the results. Resisting life. Thinking that one outcome is good, and the other one is bad. Doubting that the action being done is good enough since the ego-desired outcome is still at question. Attachments, attachments, attachments… Humans love attachments because their happiness depends on them. What they don't realize is that wishing for one outcome is resisting the flow of life, and the flow of life is always in our favor. Whether we are able to see it now or later down the road.

Peace is not about finding the silver lining in everything. Some confuse the concept of peace with being positive about everything, but it is not. Peace is an awakened understanding of finding the "enough" of your actions. Observing the event, responding as you can, and becoming detached from the outcome. You can pitch a sale, but you cannot control the buyer. You can love someone, but you cannot make them love you back. You can try to heal your health, but you can't control your recovery. That is a mind at peace, placing the energy and our efforts on the parts of life that actually belong to us. Results belong in the future, and when your mind is focused on results, you take energy away from your actions in the present.

We are wired to only feel safe when "we know" what is going on (when we have the illusion that we know what is going on). We are not comfortable stepping into situations without understanding what the outcome could be. We have an incredible fear of the unknown, so we would rather live in the illusion of "knowing" what's ahead. It is an illusion because we will never know what the future holds, no matter our plans and preparation. Anyone in doubt about this statement can look to their life events in 2020.

The moment that you make up your mind about something, you stop learning about it. You label an event as good or bad, and you immediately attach to a desired outcome. In order to be at peace, you need to have a little bit of room for life to show you what is next. You have to look back and see that life is always on your side, and it always ends up working out with what is in line with the highest good for all. A great friend of mine told me once that the coin has three sides: heads, tails, and the rim around it. Be that rim—be the side of the coin that is open to seeing both sides. We will keep missing the peace of life for as long as we keep putting our efforts on the parts of life that do not belong to us. We need to stop choosing sides and choose life; after all, that is what we came here to experience. Let go of this mindset that you know, and be more open to being shown. You don't have to do everything in this world; you do what you can, and you allow for the next step to show up. Somedays the outcome of events makes us feel good, and other days they hurt, but that is just the reaction we add to reality. In the flow of life, I promise you, you are the winner every day, so let go of your firm grip on life and finally be at peace.

Your Life Purpose
If you do not know your purpose yet, reading the title of this section probably stressed you out. "What is my purpose? I work at an office nine to five, and I like my job, but I'm not really happy. I just do it for the money, and

no one is benefiting from my work." Most people have no idea what their life purpose is, and honestly, I didn't even know what mine was until not too long ago. I thought my purpose was my way of making money, or taking care of myself or paying my bills. I was wrong. You may not have any idea how exactly you got to where you are and how you spend your time. By the time we begin to understand what our life's purpose is, we already have a career doing something that we selected, that sounded fun and could make us money to live. Do not beat yourself up. We all need to make a living, and I won't ask you to quit your job and go do yoga in the woods. I just want you to start becoming aware of who you are and the power you have on this earth.

Until you awaken into your purpose, life will keep getting more and more tiring, more confusing, and more meaningless. One day you will wonder if this is how it is supposed to be. That curiosity, that realization that something is not okay, is the beginning of your awakening. Defining your purpose in this life and the reason you are here in this world is probably one of the most important things you could ever do to find your peace. Our purpose defines our daily activities and the places and people that we will invest our energy in. If we are doing what we love, we will surround ourselves in a world we love, and therefore our life will have meaning and alignment with our highest good. The best result of all that, the ego dies; you are no longer at competition. You do things because you love it; you do your best, regardless of the outcome.

How do you find your life purpose? Let's start this with a deep question with many answers. What is the meaning of life? Life is our souls experiencing human form.

We are not human beings having a spiritual experience. We are spiritual beings having a human experience.
    —Pierre Teilhard de Chardin

If you pay attention to yourself, sitting in the room you are in, there is a duality. There is your physical body, which includes your mind, and then there is this *me*. It's the voice, the observer. The one that sits above your mind's constant narration of events and can even see what your mind is thinking from the outside. That is the real you. It is the same voice that has followed you your entire life. That is your soul energy that has always been and will always be. That soul energy is experiencing human form.

What is human form? More than just a physical body, your human form is experiencing emotions. We came here to feel. From the day we were born, we have been juggling with all these feelings within. The feelings of joy, sadness, peace, love, success, etc. Think about it; what are we constantly aiming for? Feelings. We work to make money, so we can feel successful. We date to feel love. We attempt to prevent loss, so we do not feel pain or sadness. The mind believes that it is aiming for material gains but in reality is looking for feelings. These material gains and society statuses are the catalysts that allow us to feel. They are different for everyone. For example, if you want a car for transportation, then you take any car that can drive you from point A to point B. If you want a car that makes you feel powerful and of high status, then you know what brand, make, or color specifically will allow you to feel that way. Your feelings have and will always be inside of you regardless of what the outside world is doing. Feeling at peace is very simple. As I mentioned before, it is tuning in to that lobby background piano and not into the chaos of the room. You will tune out from the chaos of the room when you are able to detach from your ego wanting survival and status. When you do something that brings peace to your soul. Choosing to live your purpose will be the light that shines from you, and it puts you on a category of your own. Many will benefit from your purpose, but it won't matter at that point. Purpose is an expression of the soul, not of the ego.

Too much time and energy are wasted in trying to control our feelings. We are endlessly trying to create experiences so we can feel love, happiness, joy, or peace. Also, we spend quite a bit of time avoiding the bad feelings like shame, pain, sadness, etc. The issue is we have been trying to do it from the outside in. What we do is as crazy as a cook trying to improve his cooking skills by purchasing new pots. We are trying to find the right boyfriend, girlfriend, job, house, or gym. And maybe we feel good for a little while, but for most it fades. After a while, it becomes part of the daily routine, and our minds begin searching for something else. And that is what we have been missing all along: only the things we create within ourselves will actually have roots in our soul and will last forever. Here is where life purpose comes in, the things we are meant to do that will give us peace of mind regardless of the outside circumstances. And yes, I made it plural because we have many purposes in this world. The higher understanding here is not what it is but where it comes from. Actions aligned with your purpose are callings from the soul, not responses to the world.

Your life purpose is what you do for this world. It is the things that simply pour out of you. You are so passionate about it that you think about it often, your life revolves around it, and you are always finding ways to perfect it. It is a light that will shine and needs no fuel from the outside world. The fuel comes from the divine itself.

Life is like a puzzle. Each one of us has a piece to that puzzle, and we must all put them together in order to complete it. Your purpose is your piece of the puzzle, and the world patiently awaits for you to place it every day. This is why we must awaken and pay attention to the clues leading us to our life purposes. If everyone searches for their peace, conflicts end, competition ends, and ego dies. There is enough in this world for everyone, and everyone can win. The purpose of the sunflower is to stand tall in beauty and produce thousands of seeds, which as a result has the ability to produce thousands of sunflowers. The sunflower is in no competition with the other sunflowers because it works at ease, knowing there is enough for everyone.

When I was young, playing sports was not my thing. I was not good at competition and throwing balls, catching balls, swimming fast, or hitting balls with a racket. During my younger years, my parents tried really hard to enroll me in all sorts of extracurricular activities. I got a black eye from a baseball, I almost drowned at swimming, and I would fake headaches to avoid practice. At some point my parents gave up. I was not going to be the good boy that played sports. And I won't lie: I always felt like I was less in school because of that.

As I entered my teenage years, just like most teens, I wanted to look good. I always wanted to look fit, but I didn't because of my lack of physical activity. I was a very skinny kid and many times bullied because of my fragile look. I asked my parents if I could join a gym. I started working out, and one day I decided to walk into a kickboxing class. The music sounded amazing; I remember the bass of the tribal house and the perfect coordination all the adults had. I joined the class and memorized the steps. It didn't take long before I was a front-row center student. I was so proud that finally I found something where I belonged. The beats, the steps, the cheering, and the endorphins—it was truly something I had never felt before.

Years later I moved to the USA and immediately looked for a gym and found my new classes to attend. I fell in love with indoor cycling and step aerobics. Finally, one day I took the leap and decided to try to teach group fitness as a hobby while I kept my full-time job as an accountant. It was probably the best decision I have ever made. I realized I did not just want to give people a strong body, but also to recreate and share with others what group fitness had done for me. I wanted people to feel how empowering it could be. It was probably the first time in my life I did something that brought me joy. I finally had found a piece of my purpose. I never cared how much I was paid to teach, and multiple times I have forgotten to submit my hours. Even though I value my income, I knew I have found something

I wanted to do because I loved it, and that was all that matters.

At first glance, you might think that my purpose in life is to be a fitness instructor. It was absolutely on the road to finding my life purpose. But I kept analyzing, and the more I understood, I realized that it was about sharing the experience, the feeling. It never felt like a job. And why did it mean so much to me? Because I had a personal experience with it. For me, it wasn't just a class. It was the fuel that helped me overcome an obstacle, and it gave me wisdom that now I was meant to share. The shame of my childhood of not feeling good enough for sports was healed through group fitness. I had a piece to the puzzle. I needed to recreate that experience for the hundreds of people desperately seeking a healthy way of life.

If you do not know what your purpose is, I want you to begin to look back and understand your wounds. Remember your story and see what you have had to overcome that maybe others didn't. In your darkest days, in your loneliest moments, and in your scariest times lies your purpose. Life has cornered you many times. At the time, it did not make sense, and you could not see beyond the pain. If you found the answer, if you were able to find a way over an obstacle, you were given wisdom. That is your piece of the puzzle. That is how you can begin to light up the world. By accepting who you are, owning your story, and being a light to others through the field that you enjoy.

One night I was eating sushi with my aunt, and she wouldn't touch the octopus nigiri. I asked her if she didn't like it. She responded, "I do but I saw a documentary on octopus and how intelligent they are, and now I can't touch it." Of course, I felt terrible for eating it, but then she continued. "The guy that filmed the documentary was actually a fisherman for octopus, and he stopped fishing the octopus and now lives for saving them."

Stories like that make you wonder how rigged the path is. Most of us spend our lives looking back at our story. We feel shame over our obstacles, and we think it could have been so much better if this or that wouldn't have happened. A perfect journey would have never given you the wisdom you have today. What you have considered negative in your life because there was pain, sadness, and fear involved has an entire positive side that you can choose to see instead. All your falls are unique to your journey, and that process of getting back onto your feet gave you a power, gave you a piece to the puzzle. We only appreciate what we have worked for; we see the value in the things that we didn't have before. We can tell the best stories when they are actually our stories. Your purpose doesn't need to be created or discovered. Remember who you are, and now light up the world with it. The rest will follow. Life is meant to be peaceful. If it doesn't feel that way right now, accept the feeling, observe it, and see where it takes you. It is always guiding you to your purpose.

The biggest doubts that people carry when it comes to living their purpose: Will I make money? Will I be successful? Will I be accepted? Will I be able to pay my bills? Stop and observe the fear. Take it one step at a time, and do not mix your ability to make money and your life purpose. When you find something you enjoy doing, none of that matters, and no external pressure can change how you feel. Your ability to manifest and align yourself with material gains and financial securities have nothing to do with your purpose. This is a story we need to rewrite. Your ability to live a life externally that supports your peace of mind is not related to your purpose. Your purpose doesn't have to be your way of making a living, and it has no impact on your ability to manifest material gains into your life. Purpose is alignment with your soul; material gains are in alignment with the outside world.

Alignment with Your Goals

Finding your purpose is a big step in your awakening to a peaceful journey. Once you understand a more meaningful reason to your existence, what do you plan to do with it? For most people, living their life purpose is something that is disconnected from their reality. For example, maybe you discover that you are somehow deeply attached to saving homeless dogs. It is something you believe in, it is fulfilling, and you feel at ease and peaceful when you are doing so. At the same time, you cannot see yourself making enough money to pay your bills and buying the car of your dreams while doing this kind of work. You know that the people that sacrifice their lives to rescuing animals do it for charity. You listen to your story, and just like most of the world, you silence your purpose and save it for another day. The day I have money, the day I retire, the day I win the lottery.

This is just another example of how powerful we are to control our circumstances, and how incredibly asleep we are as a society that we create a reality we dislike. Again, because *we know* that is just not possible to live like that. *We know* that there is no way you can pay your bills doing the things you enjoy. Because *we know* that it is just too risky to quit your job right now. All this thinking is another wall your mind built on its own. The wall is built out of fear. Fear of change, fear of the unknown, and fear of loss. I am not asking you to quit your job tomorrow and go save homeless dogs. But I am asking you to change your mindset immediately. Replace your "I know" by "What if." Everything in this world is possible. But you have to at the very least be open to it. It takes you the same amount of energy to expect things to work out than not. Expecting things to come through somehow opens you up to the possibility. Instead we choose to justify why not. You know why? Because we are too afraid to be disappointed and hurt. Because we must have a story that supports why our present feels the way it does and you are doing things right. We enable ourselves to live a life we do not agree with.

You exist in a universe that only has one answer to your stories, and that is okay.

Mind Story: I can't quit my job because it is the only way I can make money to pay my bills.
Universe Response: Okay.
Mind Story: I would never make enough to support my family doing what I love.
Universe Response: Okay.

Change it now. I am not asking you to become the ambassador of positivity. At the least just become neutral.

Be excited, be curious. What if. What if this would work out for me? What if I found a way to do something I love? I will find a way to make all of this work. And the universe still replies. Okay. But isn't that *okay* much more beneficial?

We are so used to human interactions that tend to manipulate one another. If I say I am fat and ugly, people will respond, "Oh no, you are not, you are beautiful." If I show my vulnerability and insecurities, people tend to respond with the validation I am seeking for. But when we talk about energetic alignment, it is completely different. Every action has an equal and opposite reaction. What you feel inside, what you communicate about your life, comes right back at you and proves you right.

Living your life purpose has absolutely nothing to do with the things and people you are able to manifest in your life. This is the key of what I want you to take from this chapter. Do not get those twisted. What you want in your life has nothing to do with what you do in this world. Your life purpose is not your job; your life purpose does not determine your income. Your life purpose allows you to live at ease and find your peace. Your life purpose starts within you, and it ends with your action. The results of your purpose in the outside world are none of your business. You are living your truth, and the truth does not need validation. Be at peace knowing that you can manifest the things you want in your life by having the right energetic alignment. Whatever you are lacking right now is more than likely your own fault. It is your job to be humble and awakened enough to admit to this and figure out what limiting belief is holding you back from manifesting the things you want in your life. And again, the journey of understanding your limiting beliefs has nothing to do with the journey of understanding your life purpose. We just got those mixed up in our wiring: the story in our head goes, I find a good job, I make money, I get things I want. And that is just a story, my friend. One more wall in your life that I suggest you start taking down.

The concept I just explained usually ruffles some feathers. For some it sounds very empowering, and for others with a stronger ego they cannot wait to prove me wrong. My response to all of you that are not ready to listen to this is this: just look around, my friend, you see people living their life purpose, yet they cannot manifest love. You see rich people, miserable at their jobs. And then you see most of this world living in poverty. The equation is wrong. Take your walls down; let go of so many beliefs imprinted on you. What could be so harmful about expecting things to actually work out for even better in your life?

Being born and raised in a developing country, I do have many limiting beliefs about money and abundance. I used to believe that abundance only came to a selected few who were lucky enough to have it. Yet when I moved to the US, I realized that it didn't necessarily have to be that way. I realized there are no realities, just perspectives, and I had the wrong one based on the society I grew up in. When I saw an economic system with bigger opportunities, I realized that I had a shot too at becoming someone regardless of where I came from.

Here is where it all begins. We all want to feel safe. We do not like taking risks and changing something that is somewhat working. We do not want to be in pain. I'll give you an example, which is true in the fitness industry. New

Year's resolution is the busiest time for the fitness industry; people decide collectively I will be fit this year. About two weeks later, after the peak of attendance of the New Year, the numbers begin to decline. What do you think happened? Pain. People feel pain. Working out is painful, you get sore, you lose your breath, and you fail in front of others. Sounds terrible. It is much easier and safer to go back to the activities I was successful at and feel somewhat good about myself. It is safer to settle than push myself through change.

Meanwhile, we keep seeing people that continue to do amazing at fitness. Their bodies are muscular, they can run for miles, and they lift so heavy. But we only see their accomplishments; we do not see so much of their journey. They got used to being uncomfortable, to being sore, to dropping a weight, and to giving up in front of others. They feel safe in the realm of trying.

Not putting yourself through painful, uncomfortable, and risky situations is the biggest part of settling. The problem with settling for less than what you know you are supposed to be doing will never lead you to peace. You can tell yourself over and over again that this is wonderful, followed by the perfect story you made up in your mind. Truth is, you keep living in this space where the grass is always greener on the other side. You have to find yourself deserving of the life you want. You have to be at peace, knowing that you have the power to manifest all you want in your life, therefore you don't have to stress, worry, fight, react, or be at fear anymore. Peace comes through living your life purpose; peace comes from manifesting the life you desire. Peace comes from responding to the calling from within your soul. Ignoring your truth makes you sad, angry, depressed, tired, unfulfilled, and maybe even throw some addictions in there. Sounds familiar?

We live in a society where being positive is rare and almost unwelcome. In order for you to embark on this journey, you might be a lonely sheep in some situations. You go out there, and you tell people "My life is great" and "I love myself," and you will more than likely hear a pin drop because no one knows how to respond to that. Guess why? It's their egos feeling attacked. The ego of most people works extremely hard to build these walls and limiting beliefs of why not. Remember, the ego always needs to win at everything, so if it is not winning, a very good story has been crafted to justify why. So now you are coming here and telling others how you are doing better and aiming for more, and that is the opposing force to that story. You are a different energy, and something must be done to bring you to their same vibration. Reaction. This is what people do, react to what diminishes their sense of self in order to make themselves feel good again.

This is what collective thinking is all about. You build your walls and come up with a narrative on why your life is the way it is and, more importantly, whose fault it is. Then you attract people with similar beliefs, and you feel even safer. Have you ever analyzed social interactions? People walk into a room, and nine times out of ten, something negative is spoken. "You are never going to believe this…" "Did you see what Karen was wearing…" "I read an article about the economy, and I think things are headed to a bad place…"

I truly do not believe that your friends or your circle ever has a bad intention toward you. I think they want to make themselves useful and of service in your life, so they must communicate to you all the "bad stuff" you might be missing out on. They also want to see a mirror of themselves out there and feel safe. So they project their fears in the hope that you relate, and they feel like what they are thinking is right. On that same note, sometimes we feel like people are mean because they single out our flaws or say hurtful comments. It goes in line with the same concept: people, consciously or not, need you to vibrate at the same level as them. Remember, what I am able to see in you, I have already been able to see it in myself. The outside world we see is the closest representation of what is happening inside of our minds.

I do this experiment with my dog often. Sometimes he raises his ears like he heard something and looks at me with panic. He is seeking validation: did you hear that? And if I tell him "Go get it!" he runs barking. Just like my dog, sometimes we feel things inside to the point that they seem real, but the moment we get validated by someone else, it feels like reality now, it feels good, it feels right. Unfortunately, society most of the time is ready to validate your negative stories, but not many are willing to validate your positivity. When you embark on a journey of more positive beliefs, you will feel that maybe sometimes you are alone, or maybe the key is to keep some of your most treasured dreams and desires silent. Keep your positivity away from people that do not share your visions or tend to be negative.

There is nothing wrong with negative people. They are still asleep and wrapped in their own mind and story. I believe everyone's awakening comes sooner or later, and also after an awakening, we could very easily fall back into a negative pattern. This journey is about you, taking care of yourself. Please remember that just because you are positive and have a vision for more in your life, does not make you more or less than others. If you fall into this trap of seeing where you fall in regard to others, you are still part of the game of the ego. Seeing yourself as more or less is comparison, and comparison comes from fear, and fear is a negative feeling. You take away the power of this entire experience by making it about being better than others. Awakening is listening to your calling inside, finding yourself deserving of it, and manifesting it. It never involves anyone else. Anthony de Mello in his book *Awareness* describes how someone asked him once if he was enlightened. And he is response was "Why does it matter?" Do not make the awakening process an identity; do not look around to see who is awakened or asleep. The answer is to stop labeling, to stop searching, to stop finding your place in society. This entire process is about you, only you.

The answer has been sitting right there in front of you all along. You have been manifesting up to the level of your consciousness. Listen to yourself speak. The words "I know" are some of the most dangerous words in your vocabulary. We use them for the wrong reasons. Oh I know I don't like it. I know this won't turn out good. I know that's not possible. Please stop that and change it immediately. I know this will turn out good. I know something good is in store. I know someway, somehow it will all work out. We spend hours thinking and talking about the gloomy days ahead. And we forget often that who we are today creates our circumstances tomorrow.

It is so easy to want something in the future and live your present doing the complete opposite. You want to be rich, but you do nothing to put any money away today. You want to lose weight, but you are too tired today to get a workout. You want someone to love you, but you see yourself in the mirror and dislike who you are. It is almost like we believe that the universe or the energy of the universe is going to feel bad for us or something. Wouldn't it be great for the universe to see you at the mall racking up your credit cards with expenses and saying, "Oh I feel bad for her, let's make her rich," or sitting down on your couch watching TV and eating chips and the universe says, "Let's make her fit, she deserves it, she is tired." No, absolutely not. The energy of this world responds to the nature of your song. You have to start becoming what you want, with whatever tool or small action you can take today. If you have no action to take today then start a vision board, start journaling, start affirmations, but start. We keep waiting for a better day when we have more time, when we are less tired, when we have more money; and you will find that the day never arrives. You are not really waiting for a better day; you are simply making an excuse to make yourself feel better about your present. The illusion that you will make things better tomorrow makes you feel safer with your nonaction today.

How did the ant eat the elephant? One bite at a time. Your gestation period for your goals to materialize begins today, and it is your behavior and feeling that will lead you there. Take your small steps with joy and pride in the right direction. *Maybe* is saving five dollars on a snack that you could have at home; *maybe* is a thirty-minute walk that burns you a few calories. It doesn't matter how small it is; any action is beaming your light at your goals and holding it still so the path is clear. The universe doesn't care about what is best for you. The energy field in this world just listens to you, and it is always *yes* or *yes*. Your reasons of *why not* will prove you right, and your reasons of *why yes* will prove you right as well. You are more powerful than you think. Believe it's possible, and do what's available for you to start heading in the direction you want. More importantly be patient, stay positive, and stay faithful.

Start by having a clear vision of what you want. And see your vision as something delicate and fragile. Keep it to yourself for a bit. Let it become something tangible in your life. Do not let people put unnecessary opinion on it. Remember, what you see no one else can, so you will have to be your own validation for a while. Then find the steps to do today that could help strengthen that vision. Take your little bites. Remember that a positive mindset is everything. Only speak about it as a yes. Always believe that it is already here; it just hasn't manifested in physical form. Be happy, not worried. There is nothing to worry about when you are doing something to get the things that you want. This is your moment. Most importantly, and please read this many times, do not let your happiness depend on the things you are attempting to manifest. If your happiness depends on it, you are not manifesting something you desire; you are trying to manifest something to give you the illusion that you are healing from an internal pain. Nothing outside of you will give you lasting happiness.

The person you want to become is not in denial of the person that you are today. The person you want to be tomorrow embraces where it comes from. Feel the gratitude for who you are today. Feel complete and happy where you are and from that good space, then allow for preferences and desires. It is only because of the hard work, the lessons, and the healed wounds that you are aware of what you want in your life. It is not that you are going to be better; it is simply that you are deserving of more. Love yourself for who you are today as hard as you love the person you aim to become. Don't forget that they are the same person and both are complete, worthy, and deserving of love.

Your Words Have Power

As I mentioned before, the feeling of peace is like clear and calm water. Living your life with purpose, finding yourself deserving of the things you want, and being in alignment with your goals keeps you in that space of calmness. It keeps the water settled and clear. That peaceful feeling can very quickly go away, depending on your internal conversation, meaning the voice you have in you. Handle yourself with love and compassion. Awakening to peace has a lot to do with the conversation you are having inside. The power of words is something that we underestimate. Awakening is observing this internal conversation and realizing how supportive or destructive you are being to yourself. I know that for myself it has been one of the hardest things to change. For years the conversations I had with myself were some of the most insensitive and non-compassionate talks I had with anyone. It doesn't matter how much you know about your desires and life purpose. If you keep polluting your internal environment with negativity, you will keep living a story where it is never good enough. Here is what it comes down to: if you cannot see good things in your life right now, I can promise you that even the day you make it to the body shape you want, the amount of money you want, the life you dreamed of, you will miss it. There is good in you right now, and in order to find peace we need to train your mind to recognize it and speak positive things about your life.

Whether we say it out loud or we say it silently in our minds, words have power. Words are not tangible, and they are seen as something that disappears once thought or spoken. We have the ability to apologize and sometimes say things all over again. But just like actions, words can be fixed but never forgotten. The things we have said that have made someone feel loved or hurt have been imprinted in their minds forever. Yes, time heals everything, and some things are forgotten from the conscious mind. But the trauma caused by words will always remain and show up many times in your life path.

Recently, more studies have proven that our behavior as an adult is related to our traumas as a child. Therefore, a lot of adults in recent years have begun to explore the damage done by others in their past to understand some of their responses to present circumstances. No therapy will be able to erase our past, but we can certainly find ways to understand it and cope with it better. As previously discussed, our past can be our best resource to find our strengths and wisdom and potentially our life purpose.

Life purpose comes from you and spills into the world. Your energetic alignment comes from you and manifests your desires in the outer world. They both influence your awakening to peace. Now the relationship that you have with yourself is the one that determines your inner peace and gives you the ability to stay centered through sunny and rainy days. How you speak to yourself will never have contact with the outside world, but it has enough power to block you from living your purpose and manifesting your desires. Have you ever been to a great business that suddenly closes? Then you find out that they closed not because of lack of success but because the leaders internally couldn't get along. This is why your relationship with yourself is so important. You can find your purpose, you can have all the potential to be headed for success, but if you are internally broken because of pain inflicted in you from the past, your internal world will never be able to sustain your growth. You will make some progress in life but always go back to your comfort zone, which is giving in to your fears, to what you believe to be true about who you are.

You come into this world and you love yourself. You are a pure essence. The damage begins when trauma begins to happen. Learning how to compare yourself to others. Being told that what you did was wrong. Being rejected for who you are. All of those are traumas that the outer world will put you through. You can identify them, understand them, and move forward from them. But what no one can really see is how you will continue to speak to yourself after that. Your inner talk is where the healing needs to happen. You can get over the day your first-grade teacher told you, "Your homework is not good enough and you need to redo it." But it takes a lot of attention to your unconscious mind that, now as an adult, the feeling of shame after that small event in first grade. As an adult it now translates into "Do not apply for that job because your work is not good enough," or "do not speak up about your truth because you are probably wrong." As silly as it sounds, you will be amazed by how stuff that happened years ago has an effect in your present adult life.

Understanding the events that hurt you in your past is important. I do not mean to underestimate that process, but it should be used as a tool to see how it has affected your relationship with yourself. It doesn't just end with knowing what happened—that tends to make someone a victim of their past. We need to dig deeper: yes, this happened to me, I understand it, I see how that storm passed through my life. Now ask a bigger question: how do you see yourself after that storm? How are you speaking to yourself or about yourself since that happened? What kind of walls or trust issues do you live with since then? And that's where the growth is.

It is like going back to that childlike energy. Going out there and observing children for a little bit. Little girls see themselves as princesses and young boys as superheroes. In their own imagination, with their own superpowers, they conquer all their missions. What happened to that princess or superhero in you? Who turned off your flame and showed you that you couldn't? Anytime you see yourself resisting something, or reacting to something, always ask yourself—why? Why is this bothering ME? When was the first time this bothered me? You will be so amazed to find out that at some point early on, some figure in your life forced you into this way of thinking.

You want to manifest stronger love relationships in your life. You want to have a better income. You want to have fulfilling friendships and relationships with those closer to you. You want to live a life in line with your purpose and not in line with your job. That is maybe a short list of some of the more common goals we have. Have you paid attention to how you speak to yourself in these areas?

For example: I am the first person to realize I have gained weight or I am bloated. And the minute I realize it, I see myself sabotaging my internal energy. "You should not be eating anymore today." "I cannot believe you are so dumb—well knowing what your fitness goals are, you would eat pizza for dinner."

Anytime I spend money on something I wanted for leisure or a new outfit: "This is why you don't have enough savings. You spend money in stupidity."

You start picking up on little swords you keep throwing at yourself all day long. "I don't want to go out, I hate people." "I love being alone, I can't stand people talking to me." "Ugh, I hate work." "I'd rather starve than look like that." "I look like a sausage in that dress."

I know it can be funny to joke around like that. Trust me, I have a pretty dark sense of humor. But you have no idea how much your thoughts act like a wave that demolishes a sandcastle at the beach. All your hard work, inner work, energy alignment, and taking positive action comes to a complete stop when you stop seeing your worth. As silly as it sounds, when you speak negative about yourself and you laugh, it still comes from you. It is coming from the depths of your soul, and I hate to tell you this is exactly how you feel about yourself. It is a joke with a lot of truth behind it. If you thought about it, it has a source in you.

You do not think you are good-looking enough, you are deeply afraid of people because they have hurt you in the past, you realized you could not be a princess or super-hero so you chased a career path you dislike, and you see a sausage when you wear that dress. Every word has truth hidden within; every "joke" is not just a joke.

So just like lava that comes from the depths of the earth and shows up unexpectedly, these thoughts are coming from within your soul. So we have to find a way to send something down there in the opposite direction. Almost like water to quiet down the fire within, so we can begin to heal. The universe is paying attention to your energy every instant you are alive. The universe doesn't know what is good or bad for you. The universe doesn't think you need a boyfriend, or if you cry enough it's going to make you fit and skinny. The universe really doesn't even listen to you. It is simply responding to your energy. Remember this from our alignment talk, the universe just replies "okay." You are always a winner in this lifetime.

The power of your word in your life is by far the most important thing you can have a grip on, and you should start doing that right now. Before you try to change your eating habits, and go on a yoga retreat to find out what your life purpose is, you *must* change how you speak to yourself. The power of your word is the one thing that will open a gateway in your life, or will hold you back no matter how much you try to accomplish on the outside.

Become your number-one fan and practice affirmations every day, even if it's for just a minute. Trust me, I know it can be awkward but see it as a self-love practice. Carry on with your day as normal and make sure to observe and put an end to any sabotaging thoughts about yourself. Be compassionate and gentle when speaking about your life whether out loud or in your mind. If you don't agree with your actions or any part of who you are, please be gentle with yourself. You know your journey better than anyone else. So rather than making judgments, ask questions and understand why or how you got here and create space to try again. Find the source of these claims you make about you. I promise you a lot of this way of thinking is not yours. This is all accumulations of people telling you who you are and what you need to be. If I were to reset your software right now, you go back to loving yourself, to believing you can do anything, and you need absolutely nothing in order to be happy. That's who you really are, and that's what you are aiming to go back to.

Here are some good affirmations I use on myself. Please read this like you are speaking to your own soul: I am trying my best, I am proud of myself, I am happy no matter the circumstances, I am smart, I am confident, I resolve adversity with calmness, I manifest people that love me for who I am, I am fun, I am independent, I am ready to live the life of my dreams, I am lovable, I am deserving of healthy and loving romantic relationships, I am healthy, I am healing, I love every part of me, I am capable of manifesting all I want, I am abundant, and I am living my best life today and every day.

For some of you, it might feel awkward to read that. Hint, hint. I bet you can guess what's going on deep inside that soul. That resistance you felt in some of those is exactly where you need to start asking questions. Why? Do your homework. Your words are your superpower. Through self-talk, you will find every answer that you seek, you will fix every wound from the past, and you will align yourself to manifest all you want. Use words wisely.

A World of Polarities

Awakening to peace is realizing that peace is here all the time. As I mentioned, finding your purpose involves you being able to see the positive that is hiding in your darkest times. Being able to see that all the positive wisdom that you have today that drives your life purpose came from what was once considered negative. We live in a world of polarities, a world that always needs to be in balance. The amount of positive you can perceive in a situation has an equal amount of negative impact somewhere else, and the negative times have an entire other side that is equally as positive.

We love to label things. From the day we became aware of our human form, we have been taught to label things. This is Mom, this is Dad, that's a dog, etc. We learn names for everything, including our own selves. At first, we even begin to think that who we are is our name. Labeling becomes the main purpose of our lives and our biggest learning curve. So it is no mystery that we also learn to label events. We consider events good or bad. And a lot of that is attached to the views of the society we live in. What is considered good in this country could be bad somewhere else.

So how is this a tool for awakening into peace? I like to think about it this way. There is good hiding everywhere. I know some of you reading that immediately react. There is no way you can tell me there is good when someone dies of cancer. I believe there is. I just think our minds have not been trained to look at it. Learning how to find the good in everything could be one of your biggest steps to being an awakened person and, more importantly, being able to go through life at peace.

Discussing death is absolutely pointless. Death is inevitable; we will all perish from our human form at some point. Now this is important to point out: the sadness of death is related to a loss of a person, it is equivalent to the attachments we have to what we are losing, but it is not toward death itself. We do not resent death because it's one thing we know we will all get a turn at. But still, one of the hardest things to process is how can something positive be hiding in the event of someone suffering from a deadly disease, for example. We choose to look at the pain that person is going through, and we choose to look at how their physical deterioration begins to happen. Yes, I agree that is for sure the negative of that event. Have you ever met someone going through a terminal disease? The person understands how simple life can truly be; families come together. The person lets go of most attachments and focuses on loving others. Forgiveness happens. And the people that have been close to death describe it as an incredible freeing experience. The people that are dying give up on their ego. They understand that the competition with the outside world is over, that there is no need to impress anyone anymore, and there is no longer need to fit in or be better at anything. The people closer to death have the best understanding of what life is truly about. That mastery itself is about the most positive thing that could ever happen to you or me.

I know this is a hard pill to swallow, but I promise you it works that way. We are made up of energy. We are the results of positive and negative polarities coming together. Everything in this universe happens in absolute balance. We just have stories in our head. We are programmed to react, and I guarantee you that 90 percent of the time your reactions are simply the way you were taught to react to that specific event. Imagine someone singing happy birthday at a restaurant, and when they are done, most people clap without even being part of the birthday event. It is programming. In some instances, it's harmless, and in others it is a huge obstacle.

The obstacle usually happens when something is perceived as a negative, and we go down in a spiral of negativity. One of the recent events that proved that was the pandemic in 2020. What was considered the end of an economy and a global disaster had a flip side that was not talked about enough. It was the first time the top of the Himalayas was visible from the lower grounds. In Australia, animals were roaming the streets because of the lack of vehicles. Families had never spent so much time together; some people were even saying what used to be a dining table used twice a year became a daily use during the quarantine. So yes, a huge impact to the world's economy. Many companies and people at a financial loss. But so much gain on the other side. Six months before that, the global economy was thriving, and many people were making money yet the pollution of that economy was hiding the Himalayas and keeping animals secluded and families apart.

Emotions are also polarities. Happiness and sadness, joy and pain, peace and restlessness. Too much of any emotion is never the healthiest thing you can do for staying in an awake state. Emotions work in the form of a zigzag— what goes up must go down, and what goes down must go up. And you can observe this in you. I am certain you have had periods of extreme joy and excitement, and then it progressively quieted down. At the opposite end, you might have experienced some dark moments and at some point raised to see the light. All that zigzagging keeps taking your life out of focus. You want to be awakened to peace daily. Peace is like still water. When the water is still, you can see through it with clarity. Emotional changes keep shaking up the water, and you keep losing the focus. Understand that no emotional state can be sustained forever and reduce the zigzagging. Close your eyes and feel the gratitude, and embrace the happy moments. Close your eyes, and observe the pain and lessons left by the sad moments. Happy or sad, in joy or in pain, observe the emotions and let them pass. Stay true to your purpose, and stay awakened into your peace.

At times, awakening to your peace is not work that you can do just on your own. You will encounter situations in which you want to react to something that is happening outside of you. Your life will find ways to test how truly peaceful you are with who you are. The best example I can give you is someone speaking negatively about the political party of your choice. No matter how detached we become from the outside world, some parts of us will still need to come to light and make choices in the outside world. People will challenge you and question you and make your ego become compromised. You will learn multiple times in your life that your truth does not need to be defended. You can speak your truth but never in the form of a reaction or an argument. When in doubt, wait; when in doubt, remain silent. Your truth is only meant to be spoken, and it should never have the intent of changing someone else. That is the game of the ego. I know at times it is tough, but always remember that you cannot change others; you can only share your light. What is best for you right now is peace, and peace only comes when we don't react. Reacting and responding to someone that is blinded by the inner pain just feeds the fire and continues the narrative. The truth simply is, the truth has no other version. Only those that are doubtful of their own truth are out there seeking validation or trying to change minds. The people that are desperately seeking for argument or spreading negativity are in a place of fear; they are scared that their truth might not be so true. Their ego needs you to see what they see, so they can feel safe again. We all agree that the sky is blue, and if I ever wanted you to believe that the sky is green, I would have to make a lot of noise to get your attention. At first you wouldn't be bothered by this argument and keep walking, but if people start believing me and I get you to doubt yourself, all that means is that now your truth is being compromised and you don't feel safe in your truth anymore.

We choose to look at one side of things because we must label it as good or bad. I want you to change that mindset. I want you to begin to live life in the middle, in the gray area. I want you to stop reacting. Reacting to something means your ego is leading the way. And when the ego is attached, it must decide whether a situation is beneficial to its survival or it is acting against it. Detach from your ego, detach from the situation, and simply be. You are always an observer. Your aim in this lifetime is to be at peace with your life. In order to accomplish that, you must shake hands with the present as often as you can. Smile if it calls for it, cry if it hurts, but overall accept it for what is. When I have trouble accepting something, I always quietly whisper to myself. "This is God's doing, and it is perfect in my eyes, and like everything else, it will pass."

Awakening to Love

So many of the things we are able to do right now we have learned throughout our lifetime, but the one thing we have known all along is how to love. Love is by far our most powerful instinct, and we have been using it from day one. From the minute we began to experience human form, we started falling in love with everything around us. We loved those that provided and all that surrounded us; without knowing any better, we just innocently gave love. We all have different journeys, some learned hard lessons in love too early in their life, while others have had loving journeys all along. My goal with this chapter is to show you that part of living a spiritually awakened life is to be aware that you are made out of love, that your goal is always to love, and that love is present in your life right now. When you understand how much love is present in your life and you channel it through your being first, you will be able to love those around you even more. You have in you all that is needed to fuel your life and love all that's around.

The interesting part about love is that most people think the love we receive has nothing to do with the love we give. These two are directly equivalent to each other, and the love you receive only comes from one source. That love will always come from your own self. The outside world gives you the illusion that someone else loves you, but they only love the parts of you that you have already fallen in love with. Understanding love is like searching for a lost treasure, just to come and find out that it has been with you all along. Just like peace is about rewiring your perception of life and having that aha moment and realizing that the endless search, the disappointments, and the lack of fulfillment are simply redirecting you. It is not that you haven't found where you belong; it is simply that you don't realize that you already are where you belong. Just open your eyes and see that nothing can ever come from the outside; the answers are always within. Life is always speaking to you, but we don't listen when it is so noisy outside.

We are not meant to be alone, and once again I prove my point by looking at nature. Animals love companionship; even in the wild you see them travel together, eat together, and sleep together. They help each other, they are stronger when they do things together, and they support each other in living their purpose. We are part of nature, and we are meant to do the same. Whether you stay at home alone, or you are a social butterfly, you are still part of a society, and we live in a support system. We feel better when someone tells us we are doing great, we enjoy receiving a compliment, and we heal by the energy transfer of a warm hug. We are meant to have companionship.

One of my favorite documentaries ever made is *March of the Penguins*. I cry every single time I watch it. One of the parts that is so enlightening to me is when the penguins find their mate. They hug and caress each other before making love. They embark on the journey of keeping their egg warm. They travel miles to go feed just to come back and find their mate and exchange roles. They go through a harsh winter together and try their best to give their baby a fair start in this world. Some fail and most succeed. When the babies are old enough, they go back to the shore, their mission is complete, and now they go as a group and enjoy life swimming and fishing. Just to do it all over again next season.

I do not think anyone could explain love better than my friends the penguins. That's what it is all about! Yes, you are made to be with someone and feel great. You could embark on the journey of a family and do your best with love being the driving force of it all. You will stay together for as long as you two have a journey of growth together. But you can still go to the ocean and fish and feed on your own. If the journey ends, you still go back to swimming the ocean and living your happy penguin life. Love never compromises who you are. Love never makes you a different person. You are meant to feel like you belong every day of your life because the love for yourself is present every day of your life. The love of someone else shows up in our lives just to make us even better than we are on our own.

Maya Angelou produced a video once called *Love Liberates*. She talks about her mother and how she had unconditional love for her and always encouraged her to be the best at all she did. She only gave her thoughts of encouragement and liberated her to believe she could be one of the greatest women to walk this earth. Maya actually became a great woman and left a big legacy behind. She credits her mother's love for allowing her to believe that being someone was possible for her. Maya describes love as a liberating force. Because when you love someone, you want them to be their best, whether it involves you or not. True love just wants growth; true love just wants what is best. True love doesn't want to control another person, change them, or transform them. Just like finding peace, we are light that lights a path, and people can join or leave as they please. We wish some will stay longer, but our love liberates. We liberate others to live their truth because we must live ours as well.

The society we live in is still struggling to grasp all of that idea. We define love as something we need to have in our lives in order to get married and start a family. We define the age that we should be expecting for love to happen. We see someone as incomplete for not being able to manifest love in their lives. Our egos are part of the entire journey of finding a love that defines us to be a better person than the rest of the world. The concept of love in the world we live in is completely twisted. You hear phrases like "I am looking for my other half" or "The person that completes me." This belief system gives love the sense that it is something that is hard to find, and we must find it in order to fulfill our role as a human in this society. The concept of love is very simple. You already have love, and you come to love. Love is nothing we get in this lifetime. Love as you please, and more importantly, love yourself. If you ever find one or thousands of people that love you back, then great. But you already possess all the love you need in this life. Open your eyes: people are not suffering because someone stopped loving them or because no one loves them. People are suffering because they don't know how to love themselves.

The only love you need is the love you have for yourself. Love is always there for you to feel and make you feel safe. Love is a healing energy that shows compassion and empathy for who we are. Love doesn't judge; love accepts and supports. You are the product of love, and you are meant to be in love. When I was young, I attempted to learn circus acrobatics. At the time my coach filmed a video of my tricks. When I saw the video for the first time, all I could see was my mistakes. I was young, asleep, and I wasn't very in love with who I was. Not too long ago, I found the video inside an old box. When I saw it, tears of joy came to my eyes. All I wanted to do was to hug the person in the video and tell him how amazing he was. I have missed so many special moments of my journey beating myself up, calling myself names, and being such a critic. Today I love myself, and I even found the voice in me to write this book. I want you to open up your mind and let me show you how easy life becomes when you awaken to love. When you are awakened to love, you will demand less from this world and yet receive more from it. Let's stop missing so many important days of our lives waiting for an answer that never seems to come, and turn inward and start enjoying the treasure that is lying inside each one of us.

Deserving of Love

You can only give away the things that you already have. If you have ever loved anyone around you, then love lives within you. The love that you give to others is like the flower that blooms and everyone can see. But the love within you is like the root of that flower. The outer world cannot see it, but it is what makes it possible for the flower to exist. Awakening to love is just like awakening to peace. There is nothing to search for; love already lives within you. It is a matter of learning how to feel love often on your own and not depending on the world to tell you what is to love about you. Awakening to love is looking at yourself in the mirror and opening your eyes, realizing that the person you see deserves to be loved. The person you see in the mirror gets taken for granted a lot by your own self. That person is always there, so we forget to take care of it. Ask yourself this for a moment: do you see yourself as deserving of love? All answers are valid, and remember, the beauty of me asking these questions is that only you can hear the answers. I encourage you to be honest to yourself. Most people pause for a bit before they answer a doubtful yes.

It feels weird to love yourself; it feels different to love yourself. One, because self-love is almost like a given, meaning, like, "of course I love myself, why wouldn't I?" And second, we are not quite sure what self-love means. Self-love is very simple. If you have ever been in a relationship, you probably contact that person daily, you fix yourself to see them, you remember special dates, you pay compliments, and you surprise them with a special gift. Self-love is no different. It is simply applying everything that we can do for others to ourselves. The interesting part is that we believe we learn how to love others and then we apply that to ourselves. That is actually completely wrong. You become aware of how you love by seeing how you treat others at a conscious level. Awakening to love is realizing that what you see in others you saw in yourself first. Awakening to love is acknowledging that the depth of love that you will be able to give to another is directly equivalent to the depth of love you are able to feel for your own self. Now do you see the importance of finding yourself deserving of love?

After years of figuring what the right balance is for a relationship, this is the piece that probably holds the biggest power. It's where the energy finally gets aligned. The world can only see the parts of you that you love first. If you don't think you are deserving of love, you are like the flower that never blooms. Remember that the love that you give comes from within you, and it is equivalent to the love you are feeling for yourself.

I grew up with a lot of insecurities. I knew I was gay from a very early age. The first recollection I have of being gay was when I was attending kindergarten. Looking back, it is quite interesting because kids that age do not understand sex or anything like that. It is simply that you like different things than the rest. The biggest issue is that there are not many people who are openly gay around you when you are growing up. So you have a very young mind trying to piece together a different calling in life that no one else around seems to share. No one teaches you how to be straight; your instinct takes you there, and you can be a role model for the people around you. Being gay is the same, except you don't have anyone to role model after.

At some point in my childhood, I picked up this ideal that men that took care of their bodies tended to be gay. It must have been something adults said around me. But my mind craved for something to role model after, and I became obsessed with the idea that this was what was going to lead me to finding more of my own kind. I became obsessed in my teenage years with working out and making myself a fit and muscular guy. Working out brought me so much confidence, but at the same time I started identifying with my physical results. It worked! I started liking my body, and some guys started liking me. So again, I had a story in my mind, and I validated it into my existence. Years went by, and fitness has become part of my life, but as I got older I realized that not many of my lovers have truly loved me for who I am at my core. They have failed to see the person I am inside. And bingo! That was when my awakening happened. I have manifested the same story multiple times. People come to me because of my physical appearance. I need to look good in order to be loved. My romantic partners have only loved me to the depth that I have been able to love myself. At the same time, I realized how I behaved any time I started to like someone. I usually increased the amount of working out I was doing. I would start dieting, tanning, getting my eyebrows done, getting my hair done, etc. As much as self-care is important, pay attention to why you are doing it. When you take care of yourself a little bit more when you are around someone you wish to impress, guess what? You don't think you are enough, and you believe that people should love you for your body, your hair, your eyebrows, your weight etc.

Can you relate a little bit maybe?

We live in a society that thrives on appearance. By all means, self-care is so important: working out, eating right, and loving your body like your temple. But how much of you thinks that the way your outer shell looks is the reason you will be loved? Society is completely asleep in this process because we keep proving this story to be true. I look good and people come my way. I take care of myself, and I receive praise. But just like me, it could take years before you become aware that something is missing. How come no one ever loves me the way I want to be loved? How come no romantic partner has ever seen all the special things that make me a person? Because they never came to you for those reasons. Because you do not highlight that about yourself. Because you are aligned with your looks, your body, your social status, your hair, or whatever identity you have going on; but not enough alignment is happening with the person you are inside: your story, your wounds, the obstacles you went through, your strengths, your weaknesses, or your weird habits. It is just too vulnerable to show.

Why is it so painful? Why is it such a big step for people to show who they are on the inside? Is it the fear of rejection? Just like myself developing an identity at a young age with physical appearances to welcome the fact that I was different. Can you see if you have an identity as well? We are terrified to show the person inside, to show the things we enjoy, our silly hobbies, our habits when we are down, the things we struggle with. And again, we are going to polish ourselves for that first date and present the story we feel safe telling. And if we are lucky enough to turn that into a relationship, you will potentially end up not having fulfilling love again. If you are already in a relationship, then this could be your problem too. You might have someone next to you who you enjoy. But maybe there are still items that are missing. It is okay. It is simply about becoming aware of the fact that this is who I am, and this is how I want to be loved.

You become aware that something might be missing. You become aware that maybe not showing who you are is what keeps manifesting unfulfilling relationships. But the good news is that all of this is 100 percent under your control. You are deserving of love. I am deserving of love. If you do any affirmations, please do that one at some point throughout your day. Just like any relationship you have outside of you. You are in a relationship with yourself, and it requires some daily maintenance. You cannot keep waking up every morning and forgetting about you. This is when the crazy kicks in, but you have to do it. Look at the mirror, compliment what you see, say "I am deserving of love," treat yourself with kindness, speak words of validation, and be proud of who you are today. This is who you are, you are deserving of love, so fall in love with yourself. It is not going to happen the other way around. You have to do it first. In this game we call life, you always have the first move. What you see in you first, the world can see next. Just how we discussed in alignment, the outside world simply holds the mirror up and shows you what you have already seen. The love you really want to manifest is the one that is real. It's the person that can see you for your light, for your purpose, for your strengths. Yes, attraction is a thing, and you can be drawn to the physical appearance. I promise you, though, that you will understand what falling in love is when you are next to someone that just gets you. And for that, you must show what lies under your skin. You must show what your heart is made of. You must remember who you are and love all of it.

Analyzing the behavior of children is a great way to lead us to where we are supposed to be in life. Children come into this world with a pure essence of life. They do not identify with their looks or bodies. They do not have social demands on how to behave. The imagination is flowing, and they appreciate each other for who they are. It is the job of adults to help children start fitting into society, but children they get silenced when they scream. Games are brought to an end because it is bedtime. Diets are enforced to prevent being overweight. Some children suffer too early with adult stories that are handed down to them like death, divorce, loss of money, etc. Basically, the mind starts getting shaped as we grow up. Anytime the child is corrected, more of that natural flame shuts down, and the mind is put to sleep more and more. The mind learns to please the instructions coming from the outside and to respond less to the callings of the inside. Little by little the person inside is forgotten. The child learns to live for praise for his actions, praise for what the world can see and validate and not from what's inside. Each time the behavior of the kid is fixed, a bruise is left in the mind that will turn into a trauma that will accompany that person for life. The intention of our parents and role models is to help us fit into society, which is necessary. But now that we are adults, we must turn around and speak to that child we left behind on us and tell him he is special. Tell him he still exists. Tell him it is his turn to be loved. You already know that you can't scream in a restaurant and that you should get eight hours of sleep. So now is the time to go back and love the unique energy, dreams, and wisdom that you shut down as a child.

George Pratt and Peter Lambrou, in their book *Code to Joy*, share the story of one of their clients, who had a very difficult relationship with her own self. No matter how much joy she was surrounded with, she was always depressed. It was triggered at a young age when her family was upset at her for accepting a quarter from her aunt to do some chore work. They taught her that she should never accept money from a family member. She was very proud of doing something great for her aunt and earning some money, and it was immediately shut down by her parents, and she was told how wrong it was. This insecurity came along with her for years, and as an adult she lost the ability to relate that so much of her life events were related to this experience as a kid. She had accomplished so much in her adult life but never felt like anything she did was good enough, and it all tied back to a small incident of being put to shame over a quarter.

A great friend of mine shared with me a story that when she was young she had a Halloween party at her house. At some point in the party, one of her guests said the party was boring and that she was leaving. When she left, she brought along a bunch of other guests with her. The Halloween party was almost empty by the time they left, and they had to end it earlier than planned. My friend felt rejection and shame for her ability to entertain others. This trauma was big enough to be something to heal in her adult life when she never wanted to have anyone over for social gatherings.

When I was young, I was bullied in school because of my mannerisms. The guys that did it always did it in the hallways of school or the bathrooms. I was terrified of walking in front of groups of guys. As an adult, when I worked in an office environment, I realized that I used to wait for the bathrooms to be empty for me to get up and use them. I never felt okay getting up when other people were in the hallways of bathrooms. One day I picked up on it and did my homework to ask, "But why am I doing this?" And there it was, a childhood fear holding me back from feeling deserving in my adult life.

I am certain you have your stories too. But enough is enough. These events came your way when your mind was young and too early to process what was really going on. Close your eyes and take yourself back. Tell that kid in you that it is okay, it is safe now, you are perfect the way you are. We don't have to pretend to be anything anymore. At this point in your life you know you can provide for yourself, you can be yourself, and you can be by yourself, so there is no need to feel shame from the outside anymore.

All techniques you see out there, all therapies, retreats, and even this book itself have one thing in common. They all want to remind you who you are. We are all attempting to peel layers of emotional walls that you have built to keep your true feelings from showing. Peeling it all back to the core: the pure, vulnerable, and innocent mind you were before. Allowing you to be. We have learned that you will only be able to fully love, to fully live, when you are yourself, no one else. You are meant to cry, cheer, laugh, and feel. So much in life continues to not feel right because you are being someone who you are not. You keep struggling to manifest someone that loves every part of who you are because you are not letting the world see who you truly are. The answer is as deep and simple as, just be. Why is it so simple? Because you already are; no one needs to show you how to be you. Why is it so deep? Because you are overwhelmed with memories, stories, traumas, and trying to fit in, and you forgot how to be you. You are scared to show who you are. You have been told that it was not okay to be you.

You must find a way to just let it go. The key is to stop identifying with it. Ask yourself questions often. Why am I doing this? Observe your emotional background. How are you feeling right now? Why am I upset or sad? Is it because of a memory or this actual moment? Memories and events are just like clouds in the sky. Before awakening, it feels like those clouds do not move as fast as they should, and more often than not you have a dark, rainy cloud that sits above you for long and produces gloom all around you. We identify with it, and we keep feeding it. We keep talking about it. We are offended by it. Now that you are awakening, they will begin to move quicker. I do not believe clouds will ever stop from coming, but you will learn to observe them as they pass. It is easier when you learn to detach yourself from your story and observe it from the outside. Be gentle to yourself. Do not dismiss your feelings; observe them. Feel your feelings but also let them pass.

Your mind probably gets overwhelmed by the number of events and stories that make you up. By all means, you should spend some time identifying what needs healing from your past. But more important than that, I want you to practice, daily, the art of self-love. Yes, you have a story; yes, you have insecurities and things to overcome. But you are ready. You are deserving of love right here and right now. You need to see yourself in the mirror and be proud of what you see, what you have been through, and what you are becoming. But there is no more need to wait or pretend. Love your story; love yourself—now.

Break free from this story of "I am working on myself."
All the world hears is "I am not ready." Stop aiming to
make yourself be perfect before you allow yourself to be
deserving of love. You deserve love right here and right
now, the way you are, no matter what. And you most complete this step before you can demand to be loved for who
you are by someone else. You must see it first. The game of
love starts with the relationship between you and yourself.
Come on, you deserve it; show us who you are. Life is so
beautiful when we stop pretending and we start being. This
life is about learning to love. You must love all of you, all of
your story and your past. It made you who you are today;
it got you to this awakening point. You would have never
woken up and questioned how to be better if it weren't for
the obstacles. Your alignment has been off all this time, and
the world has perceived you as "I am not ready yet," "I have
made mistakes before," "I am still fixing myself," and "I am
not good enough yet." Today we change that. We continue
on the journey of growth and understanding the depths of
our soul. But we know that it is time to stop pretending
and just start being. Remember, it never felt right because
it was always a lie. If you want to feel true love, you must
walk into the experience with your truth, for who you are.
We own our past and our story, and we understand that
it gives us the resilience we have today. When we look in
the mirror, we see nothing else but someone that deserves
to be loved for all that was, for all that is, and for all that
is becoming. Awakening to love just made life easier. I can
finally stop wasting time trying, and I can start being. It is
as simple as "I will love every part of me, so the world can
love every part of who I am."

Falling in Love

So now we are awake enough to know that we deserve love. We understand that we are lovable. We can see the pattern that the love that we are able to give is equivalent to the love we think we deserve. We know the first step to awakening to love or cleaning the love house is really learning to love that person that we see in the mirror. Not just physically or by its outer shell, but also for the story and the past that it has been through. If you do this exercise, it will get you somewhere. One day someone stands in front of you, and you begin to observe what is happening inside of you. You are not sure why you are so complete. Your internal environment seems at peace, and all search is over. You are present. You have fallen in love.

One time I was trying to understand the concept of being present. Being in the moment. I just had trouble understanding how I could not be present if I was here physically right now doing this. A friend of mine told me, "You know you are present when you do something that lets you forget time exists." I know sometimes I teach classes and I dive so much into them, and I seriously do not understand where time goes. I am passionate about teaching fitness. I also know that the times I have been with someone I loved, hours can go by and I do not even realize where time went. That is being present. Because you simply are. Love is one of the few things in this world that will make you present. When you are with the one you love, nothing else matters. Here is something important to know, though. The mind is addicted to the activities that make it present. The mind loves getting a break. The mind is so ready to relax and stop analyzing the past and the future. So the mind loves to be in love. Love is addicting, and this is why we must be awake to fully understand what falling in love is truly about.

Let's talk about what falling in love is. It is simple: loving something or someone is pretty much acknowledging them with a deeper gratitude. If I show you a random animal, you can say, "Oh how cute." If I show you your personal pet, now there is a deeper feeling of gratitude for its existence: you want him for you, it is something that you create in your mind that makes it strong, the idea of possession and in a certain way you create an identity around it. "This is my cat." You have fallen in love with your cat at some point, and you love him or her. Same goes for romantic lovers. "This is my boyfriend." All those things are beautiful because you are feeling very strong emotions that allow you to fully express yourself. But anytime we are playing around with feelings of possession, control, or identities felt around something or someone, it is a slippery surface. Everything in life has a beginning and an end, even your own life. We must be responsible and understand what is happening within us while falling in love, so we can control our emotional state. Awakening to love is falling in love responsibly. Just like we talked about polarities. Too much happiness can cause too much sadness. We are the most efficient when we stay in the middle. Smiling with humble gratitude during the good times and surrendering to life during the sad times.

I am not going to lie; there is a phrase in love that makes me cringe a little bit. "I have finally found my forever love." You know how passionate I am about saying that we live in the circumstances of our mind-made stories. Your mind falls in love, and now you add this insane story around it: "He or she is my forever love." So now you are living in this story, and suddenly things fall apart. Well, no wonder people are terrified of falling in love. I believe that the loss of someone you love can even be harder to grieve than the death of someone special. When someone dies, the story in your head makes some sense. We know deep inside that eventually all of us will perish one way or another. But losing someone because they don't love you back, or they met someone else, that right there is devastating for the mind. And this is why there is a large group of people that have completely shut down the love house. They tried it once, and the letdown, the betrayal, and the unmet expectations were just way too painful. They never want to lose their identity like that again.

I do think we should all take a little responsibility, though, on how we have signed up for this disappointment about falling in love. You don't believe in love? What happened? What story in your head was not fulfilled? For some people, it is not even their own story; maybe it is the story of their parents. The story goes: Mom and Dad love each other and take care of their family. Then one day you come home, and Mom and Dad are in a battlefield, and one leaves the house. That's enough for someone to sign out from the game of love. On the other hand, have you noticed that the dating scene gets pretty rough at the early thirties to the late forties? Why is that? People tend to go through their first deep relationships in their mid-twenties. They meet *the one*. They entered the slippery surface. Just like before, the mind begins typing the story: on this day I have met my soul mate, my other half, and the one for me; I want to start a family, move in, save for retirement, and I am finally with my person. For some lucky ones, this story is true. I have met plenty of them, and it's truly beautiful to listen to their soul mate's love. But for another group of people, things fall apart. And when that level of high emotions, happiness, and love story is deemed to be a lie, the person will more than likely shut down. The person becomes emotionally unavailable because love hurts. So then you see them in bars and dating sites, believing that they are ready to fall in love again. And they actually are ready, but the minute that emotions begin to arise, it is just too scary. They are reminded of the trauma, and it is just too risky, too vulnerable to put their mental stability on the line again. It is more exciting to live in the story of hunting for someone unavailable or live in the misery of that person who doesn't like me, than actually diving into a fully functional relationship and being vulnerable again.

By now you probably think that I am scaring you away from falling in love. But I promise I am not. I actually want you to fall in love. If you are with someone, fall in love with that person again. If you are single and terrified of love, I want you to open up to it again. If you are single and ready to mingle, I want you to fall in love but consciously. I want you to fall in love in an awakened state. The love that hurts is unconscious love. It's asleep love. Love is like an addictive medication. Use it as prescribed; otherwise, you are in trouble. It is one of the best feelings in the world. I want you to be present, and just like living your purpose, living in love will make you present. When you live in the present moment, your life will feel more fulfilling.

What is that you look for in someone that you want to fall in love with? If you have a piece of paper, maybe write some of those things down. You probably believe that you have a type: I like a person that looks like this and that and makes good money and has a job. Maybe you like someone that validates you and tells you how cute you look before going to work. You also want someone that is loyal and thinks you are the best thing in their life. You want someone that accepts you for who you are. Maybe you want someone that wants to start a family and so on. Now here is where I am going to wake you up. Why do you want the person you fall in love with to be that way? First answer that comes to mind is probably "That's just what I like." That's valid. But go further—why? What about someone having a job or not makes that person more lovable? You might think, *Well, I don't want to support someone, I want someone who I can rely on financially.* Valid answer as well. But go even further Why? You keep telling me all the reasons why this person fits in your checklist. You are telling me what *you* feel safe next to. But you still don't tell me what that has to do with falling in love with someone else.

Oh wait a second, is that the answer again? You are looking for someone that fits in your story. Your mind made another story of what your love partner looks like and feels like. See! Your ego loves to put different costumes on. So today the ego wants to play the "let's fall in love" game. So it comes up with a list of things that a person next to you should have, and guess what? I can guarantee you that if your story comes through, and you start a relationship with this person, your relationship will be better than everyone else's. Otherwise, the ego will not be happy. Because that's what the ego does: it turns love into a fear game, into an identity of this is what we need to do, so we can get praise and validation from this world. If you want to analyze it further, just take another look at your list. How will your immediate circle react if you found a lover that met your criteria? Family will approve, friends will approve, social media will approve, and everyone is happy. So this is how the ego has played games with you and falling in love. You haven't even really been searching for actual love. Once again, you were trying to fit into the mold of society. Falling in love is something that happens in the present moment, and it just feels good in that moment. Meeting someone or going on a date with an agenda in mind is not falling in love; that is simply playing the game of the ego. I have so much hope for love when someone calls me and tells me, "Alfredo, guess what? I met an awesome person: we have the best sex, and we talk until 3:00 a.m. about really meaningful stuff. He understands me, I love the advice he gives me, and I feel I can be myself… But there's a problem. He has no job, he is buried in debt, and he transports himself on a bicycle." My response is, "Awesome!" You have fallen in love. That's it! I hope your new lover finds a job and accomplishes a lot in his life. But again, we do not have to get concepts twisted. You don't find your soul mate by reading through résumés. You find them by touching, talking, hugging, crying, and kissing. Love is an emotion, not a legal document.

Go back to your list to all the things you are looking for in a person. Wake up! This has nothing to do with the other person, and it has everything to do with you. This is why falling in love has been so confusing all along. The ego wants you to find someone that is going to make you look good on the outside and makes you feel safe for the future, which is an absolute delusion. The few times you have actually fallen in love with someone, all it took was for you to feel good on the inside, and nothing else mattered. Society has made it so confusing again because you believe that falling in love is all about what that other person is like. And now you have all these dating apps, and you read how everyone is playing a game and presenting to the world what they can do for them in their future. That is 100 percent all ego and nothing to do with falling in love.

Falling in love just happens; it's magical. It seemed, though, that anytime you have fallen in love, you thought you loved the other person. But in reality, you found someone that simply highlights the parts of your life that you have been covering all along. And when that person is gone, or when they fail to act like we expect them to do so, you are left wondering how to express parts of you to the world that you can't seem to express on your own. True love is present and is therefore liberating. True love allows you to be you and that's why no job, no money, or no car can ever be a stronger force. You only fall in love with the people in your life that make you love yourself more when they are part of your journey. Read that again: you only fall in love with the people in your life that make you love yourself more when they are part of your journey. You do not fall in love with someone else. You fall in love with yourself. You fall in love with the feelings and emotions you feel inside when that person is part of your life. And we are not alone in this; nature works like this too: your dog loves you because its life is so much fun and better when you are around. When you are around its belly is full, games are on, and loneliness is gone. The dog loves his life more when his human friend is part of it. You like coming home and seeing your four-legged friend greeting you. He cuddles you, he plays with you, and he needs you. Therefore, you love your life more when your dog is a part of it. You love your life more with your dog in it. At no point has the human or the dog transferred anything. They just appreciate each other being themselves. Both the human and the dog individually feel special and present in their own mind.

Now take it to a romantic level—you enjoy waking up next to someone. You enjoy having someone give you a warm hug. You enjoy being intimate and the feeling of making love. So many events that can make you fall in love with someone else. But see how all of those feelings are never transferred by one person to the other. All of those feelings started within us. We fell in love with us; we fell in love with what we felt inside individually. How empowering is that? You did not have to become anything to feel that way; it actually came from allowing yourself to be free.

You are probably terrified of what I am going to suggest. No, I am not going to tell you to just forget about other people and fall in love with yourself. I do not believe we have the capacity to live life at its fullest like that. I believe that the level of happiness and excitement we get doing things with someone else is very special, and we should take advantage of any opportunity to do so. Just consciously. My answers come from nature. Animals fall in love; we are meant to fall in love. We are meant to explore growth next to someone. What we are not meant to do is to lose our bearings because of someone else. We actually should fall in love more often and drop the agenda of controlling our future. Your life is your responsibility, so stop demanding that you meet someone that completes you. You are good; you don't need anyone for that. It's actually all the opposite to start loving yourself individually and attract the love from someone that takes you as you are and highlights more of who you are. Someone that appreciates your truth. I love marriages where the dad raises the kids, and the mom goes out to work. What an incredible change of dynamic. It breaks the patterns of society, and both partners allow each other to be. Husband allows his wife to go work and keep exploring her career, and he takes a different path and raises the family. It works for them. They both listen to each other instead of staying asleep through the road map provided by society. They both love each other.

The human mind is powerful and probably one of the most advanced in nature, so we need to learn how to use it properly. Feeling present, feeling good is addictive. Think of addictive pleasure that lets you feel good. Sugar is addictive; sugar tastes good for many. Moderately eating sugar is a nice treat. Eating sugar every chance you crave it will make you sick. For some people maybe it is alcohol or marijuana. A drink here and there or maybe at nights, not too much trouble. Drinking or smoking all day to the point of intoxication will probably get you into some troubles in life. Moderation, balance, and control.

When you fall in love observe it. Observe the amazing transformations that it is doing to your life. The intimate moments when life pauses. You feel so complete when that person gives you a hug. That crazy smile that just shows up on your face when the one you have your eye on contacts you. It is wonderful when you start feeling in love. Keep observing, and be aware when the self-sabotage begins as well. Your mind will probably start jumping to define it; your mind is always going to resist being present and will lean toward creating a story around it. Is he the one? Is she real? Is he going to call me tomorrow? Just quiet it down. And enjoy your moment. Even if this relationship would be guaranteed to last forever, I promise you that those moments are temporary. I also promise you the story you are building around it is almost completely wrong. Give others the chance to reveal themselves to you; see people by facts, not illusions. You are falling in love with your idea of that person, not that person itself. You still have no idea who he or she is. That might take you a couple reads to grasp it, but once you do, it's liberating.

Stay aware of what is happening inside of you. Everything that you are feeling starts and ends with you. Nothing is being given to you; nothing is coming from the outside. The other person is simply a catalyst for you to feel this special, and you are the catalyst for the other person. You can try your best to awaken the same or better feelings for them, but at the end what they feel is their responsibility, it is their individual journey, and it has nothing to do with you. What I am trying to say here is do not lose your ability to experience your experience of love by trying to manipulate theirs. All you can do is be yourself as honest and vulnerable as you can.

Allow yourself to feel, allow yourself to be present, and enjoy this treasured moment. Be aware of the volatility of the moment, and know it is temporary. Keep your power. You know that this process is simply highlighting parts of you. Nothing is being taken from you; nothing is being given. All you feel is inside of you, and it will always be there for you to feel it whenever you want.

This is the beauty of falling in love in an awakened state. You get to enjoy the beauty of loving another soul, but you fully understand that your true soul is never compromised. When you are asleep, your ego takes control of the situation. Your ego will give you the illusion that you need this person in order to be complete. Falling in love unconsciously is like becoming a parasite; you now need that other person in order to keep your growth. Awakened love shows you the opposite. You are still the same person; you are still standing alone. You are just enjoying it in a playful way, exploring your emotions through the interactions with someone else. But you are still you, it never got taken away, and it is still your responsibility to take care of yourself.

Have you noticed that some people meet and fall in love, and two weeks later they walk away? It is because it was unconscious love. They met someone for whom they were on their own. Codependency begins to happen and is either too scary, or a turnoff, and more importantly it is no longer the same two people that met on the first place. The ego is telling you that you shouldn't be alone, you should have someone else, your friends are married, and what is wrong with you that you can't have someone that loves you in your life. So almost like a predator lion, the minute that it finds someone, it jumps on it and clings to it immediately, and that is not love. That is the fulfillment of a mind story. Those little special feelings and butterflies and being present are not there anymore; now it's just an agenda that needs to be completed. You will remain the same when you hold on to your awakened state. When you realize you are the source of your life and that is never taken away. When you never forget who you are. It is okay to desire someone in your life, but your happiness is not dependent on it.

Fall in love, my friend. But fall in love with the way that person makes you feel. In return, love that person for who they are. Giving love to someone else is simple. It is gratitude. Appreciate all the things about that person that makes them so special to you. Don't try to change them. There is no need and actually no way to change someone else. Simply lead by example, and give love with no expectations. Falling in love has nothing to do with the fact that this might or might not be your life long partner. I wish I could tell you how to turn falling in love with someone into a relationship, but if I did, I will actually be giving you an identity. I will be contradicting myself. I want you to enjoy the present; the future will present itself when its time comes and you will be awake enough to handle it with grace.

You do not fall in love with someone's money; you do not fall in love with someone's desire to have kids or not. You do not fall in love with someone that can afford a house or not. Keep that separate. That is attraction that is part of all this, but it is not love. Love grows differently, and love lasts forever; attraction changes often. You fall in love with a soul that allows you to fall in love even more with yourself. And because of that you love their soul, their essence as a human back. This is the beginning of the journey, and it should be taken for what it is. Only time will tell; you stay awake enough to know that no part of you is ever compromised. You deserve love, and there is no better part of love than falling in love as many times as you can. With the same person, or maybe in the search for one that is here for many seasons. Just let it unfold in its own magical way, align yourself with your intention, and be the best you can be in this moment. Love never took anything from you, and it will not. Now wake up and fall in love more often. You are ready *now*.

Staying in Love

As a society, we constantly focus on the beautiful moments of two people falling in love. Movies are made, songs are played, and books are written about the intensity of two people meeting and desiring each other. But not much is said about the mastery of staying in love. Are we afraid of what it involves? Living awake to love is being in touch with yourself and not fearing the depth of staying in love. Asleep or unconscious love is the one that, once the excitement of falling in love is over, we are ready to move on so we can create the feeling again with someone new. This is very common in the dating world today. The ego-driven mind believes that it is searching for a long-term relationship, but once it realizes what is involved in staying next to someone, it backs out from it. It is a very special feeling the moment when someone you are attracted to is attracted back to you. It feels like it validates you in this world. Love has a bigger purpose, though, than just making you feel validated. Through the love experience you have with someone else, you will get to know aspects of yourself that you would never be aware of on your own. It is vulnerable, emotional, and sometimes painful to hold someone's hand and see parts of you that have been hidden for a lifetime. Love is the catalyst to your growth; it involves trust in someone else, and it will redefine the way you see yourself. Love brings life and presence to the person who you are with. We know we can do life alone and be masters of our own journey. But there is another side to life of us growing with someone else, which we can only explore while being in love. This is why the egoistic mind cannot move past falling in love because the ego likes to feel special all the time, and this side of the journey involves growth. The ego is never ready to see where the soul is broken because it feels diminished compared to others. Awakening to love is realizing that there comes a time that we must stay in love in order to allow someone else to show us parts of us, that we cannot see on our own. Awakening to love is realizing that part of your journey to healing past trauma is done next to someone you love. In one way or another, we have all been broken by the outside world. Since childhood, we have built trust issues, walls, and preconceived notions that have unconsciously defined how much we let others in. Remaining next to someone you love will force you to challenge all of those traumas at some point and embark in the journey of healing. As long as you remain awake and aware while that growth and healing is happening, you will stay in love for as long as it is necessary.

Keep in mind, you can start a family and a home with anyone that you get along with and share that common goal, so marriage and long-term relationships are not necessarily equivalent to love. People believe you have to be married by a certain age, and it will be nice to have a certain number of kids. Those are amazing goals to have, and you should accomplish them with someone you are in love with. Many, though, have just processed those goals and fallen asleep and confused what appeared to be love by the excitement of another checklist item fulfilled by the ego. Being in love is different: it challenges you every day, and there is emotional healing happening between both partners. More parts of you keep showing up and is a much deeper relationship that at times cannot even be defined. It's magical, and it takes place in the present moment all the time. You could decide to accomplish your goal to be married to the one you are in love with and maybe even start a bigger project like a family, but that is not the reason why you are next to this person.

The key to staying in love is losing the fear of letting someone in to see your true self. It takes trust to let someone see your hidden stories and dark sides. We all long to be healed. Remember, we all want to be at peace and one with life. In order to get there, we need to get over the trauma and conditioning that has made us the way we are. We have fears, we have judgments, and we have triggers. You might find that maybe your mind sees those things as simply "That's how I am, and that is okay." The truth is that is not really how you are. There is a belief system in you that has made you that way. No one is really an introvert. Someone made you feel small, and you enjoyed the safety of remaining quiet. No one is triggered in anger when there is too much noise. Someone in your past must have silenced you to the point that it made you react to noisy people. My goal is not to change you and make you a noisy person that loves being around people. My goal is to bring peace to your soul, and that only comes from being awake, being present. Yes, you are meant to be a certain way, but you are not meant to have judgments, triggers, reactions, or anger. You are meant to be tolerant and at ease with life. That's how love makes us grow. It breaks us from being so set in our ways and forces us to be tolerant by interacting with someone we love. Love forces you not to change but to become aware of your belief system and traumas. Through staying in love with someone, you will constantly be challenged to play with your energy in ways that you wouldn't do if you were always alone. You are with another soul, in intimate environments. You are being observed by someone that loves you on your dark days and happy days. Through that interaction, your partner holds up a mirror and allows you to see what you cannot see alone. Awareness comes to you, and growth happens. Once you are aware of your wounds and start to understand them, you begin to relax. When a feeling arises that made you react in the past, now you just observe them. You stop living in your past identities, and you begin to choose peace over war.

When you start letting someone in and you choose to stay in love, your primary role as partners is to keep building that trust so you can hold those mirrors up and show with compassion and empathy the parts that are creating pain within you. The way to build trust in a relationship is through communication. The success of staying in love is directly equivalent to the quality of the communication the couple has with one another. I use the word *quality* because there are many layers to communication. Two people can text every day about gossip and silly things and say they communicate a lot. Quality communication is a real expression of what is happening inside of us. I am not suggesting you become an open book every day. But if you are awake, you will be in touch with your feelings and emotions and be able to talk about them with clarity. A lot of people who are awake might feel like they suffer more. It's not that you suffer more; it's that you are more in touch with yourself and not hiding behind the identities of the ego. An awakened person is fine acknowledging that today might be a good day, and tomorrow they have emotions showing up. Staying in love is communicating those moments to your partner in order to build trust. It is like running a business: today I do not feel great, I am not happy with my job, and I feel lonely. Staying in love is present, and there is an honest desire to let go and to heal. In order to do that, we communicate with no attachments to the result. What I mean by no attachments to the result of a conversation is that your awakened goal is to see yourself better, but the ego could sneak in in this process and communicate pains with an attachment to people feeling bad for you. And what does the ego get as a result of that? A pity party, which results in validation. Just keep an eye out for that in order to keep your communication successful, with no agenda and in favor of staying in love.

It is your responsibility to express your needs. Unconscious love plays a game. Back to the example of "today I feel lonely." The unconscious lover will play a game.

Their partner reaches out, and maybe they do not answer the phone. In search of attention to heal the thought of today, I feel lonely. The unconscious lover is not aware of the pains and sabotages the present moment to feel better, without ever communicating the root of the problem. The unconscious lover is driven by the ego and will never show weakness, instead remaining silent and having someone try to call them ten times to feel needed. That relationship is not about love anymore; it's about control and will more than likely feel toxic and come to an end or create a lot of pain. I cannot emphasize enough the importance of communicating your needs in the moment. If you are uncomfortable today, find the right moment to let your lover know. If you don't feel right, it is simply that it is not right for you. No one can tell you what is right or wrong for you. Stop trying to hide and making yourself small, thinking that tomorrow will be better. Your issues will pile up and sooner or later will blow up on you like a piñata. Staying in love is remaining in love. If you are not happy with something, even if you are later proven wrong, you must communicate it in the moment. Otherwise, you are not staying in love. You are pretending to be in love and playing to be with someone.

Communicating your needs is the only way that growth happens. If you are not sure how your partner will receive the information, then it is a perfect tool to know if this is a relationship worth staying in love for. It always goes back to the same thought process. You do you. If you feel lonely, welcome your feeling of feeling lonely. Feel your feelings and communicate them to the person next to you. If they are awake, if they are aware like you are, they will welcome your feelings and hold your hand through it all. They will observe with you or maybe help you dive into it a little bit. Think about it. If you feel lonely, it's as simple as becoming present and realizing that you are not lonely anymore. That's all. Healing can be quick when you are awake and let your pain out. But the beauty of staying in love happens right there. When you have someone next to you that you can have deep conversations with, and no games are played. This bond seals the relationship a little tighter. Do not be afraid that because today it's your turn to communicate something painful that it makes you weaker. You set the tone, and it will be your partner's turn soon enough. We are all fighting a battle, we are all healing, and we all have something in our past that we need to talk about.

Staying in love requires you to be awake often. Partners begin to date; they might grow their relationship into a marriage and potentially even into a family. Every step of the way requires more depth and awareness. A relationship between two people might not just involve deciding to go out for a drink one night. Maybe it now involves a mortgage payment, a car payment, a grocery list, a school event, a kid going through challenges at school, etc. All of those things are part of a relationship, but they are not part of staying in love. It is your job as an individual to clean the clutter from in between you and your lover. Do not bring in between one another what doesn't belong. Remember that staying in love is about the healing and growth between the two people that fell in love. Love is spiritual, love is intimate, and love is deep. Your lover is not your business partner, not your punching bag, and not your money source. Pay close attention to the reason people get married, and pay close attention to the reason people get divorced. When they fall in love it is pure, it is real, and it is deep. When they get divorced it is superficial, it is materialistic, and it is selfish. They lost their direction along the way. They forgot what the point was. In order to stay in love, you must create the space in your relationship for love to happen. You most have the communication open and the ability to turn life off and have deep, intimate moments with your partner. That is the base of everything; staying in love is like the glue that will hold the rest together.

It is important to point out that in order to stay in love you must also remind yourself of how you got to falling in love in an awakened state. You got to that point by taking responsibility for you. By realizing that love wasn't a salvation to your soul but a compliment to your journey of healing. As time goes by you will find that codependency begins to happen. We must remain awake enough to understand that throughout our lifetime we are responsible for us. We are still responsible for our well-being, our happiness, our self-love. We still need to find that person in the mirror and see beauty. We still need to be aligned with our goals and desires. We still need to be on our own path and seeing our lover as the complement to our growth. Do not let your relationship make you small. Do not let your relationship quiet your flame. Frustration, anger, fear, control, and disappointment are just some of the few negative feelings you bring in between you and your partner when you put the irrational demand of someone else taking care of you. I do not care if you are a man or a woman, or if you are younger or older. If you want to stay in love, if you want to keep it real, and if you want this to last you never stop being the source of everything in your life. Love makes life better, love makes growth easier, but love doesn't take care of anything—we always do that on our own. It feels nice if your partner suggests you quit your job and stay home, maybe temporarily, but never lose your independence, and never stop being you. It is likely to be something you could regret at some point.

Outside challenges will always want to challenge your relationship. Here is the rule of thumb for everything I have been telling you in this book. When the outside world is influencing your internal world, you have become unconscious. When the outside world cannot change your internal environment, you are awakened. Easier said than done, I agree. But this is a daily job we have that gets easier with time. You must observe yourself daily on how you are responding to the circumstances outside of you. When it comes to staying in love, this piece plays a huge role. Outside circumstances will present themselves as obstacles in your relationship. The economy changes, and it affects our lives, health issues present themselves, and it affects our activities and demeanor. Commitments change, and our schedule changes. In summary life happens, and your relationship will face challenges. Is it worth it to stay in love? Or is it time to move on? It's a tough question to come across. But like any other feeling that arises, ignoring it will be playing a game. Remember that everything in life is temporary. Remember the reasons why you and your partner came together. Keep that alive; keep the communication flowing. Remember, the duty is mutual. Your partner is here to help you with your growth, with your fears, to hold the mirror up so you can see the parts of you that you cannot see on your own. You have the same duty for your partner. In real love nothing is given, nothing is taken; we simply hold hands and explore new depths of our soul. We become one with life by accepting more and reacting less. You might be next to this person for a month, a year, or a lifetime. Only you will be able to be aware if you are staying in love or if the purpose of the journey together has been accomplished. Both answers are possible, and neither one should be labeled as good or bad. They both simply are.

Moving On

The last piece I want to cover about being awake to love is the one that is the hardest to talk about. Unfortunately, sometimes it doesn't work out between two people. Every now and then you meet someone that has been with the same person since high school, and it is all still working great, even four decades later. That is an anomaly. For most of us, we have to go through these difficult steps many times in our lifetime. It is the hardest step because it is actually the one that requires you to be the most awake. Moving on requires you to listen to your soul and know that growth is not happening anymore between you and your partner. Relationships switch from bringing healing into your life to suddenly creating more pain. The love, empathy, and compassion for the two souls is no longer the glue that is holding it together. It is the fear of letting go; the fear of change; and the outside commitments like marriage, money, kids, etc. that is keeping it all bonded.

Here is the part that I want to emphasize for you. Listen to yourself! Honor your feelings! Feel your feelings! Speak your truth! One of the most common things you see with couples that are going through rough times or splitting is the amount of stuff that starts coming out during the process. The same concept we discussed while *staying in love* applies here. It is your responsibility to communicate your needs. Holding on to a list of emotional disappointments and letdowns of your partner, and suddenly bursting like a water pipe, is the game of the ego. You lost your awareness in the process of making your needs not relevant for the sake of your relationship. At no point does the love between two people demand that one of them should sacrifice feelings for the sake of the other. True love actually wants you to show up every day, so it can give you the love and healing that you long for. It doesn't matter if your partner is all wrong, and you are all right; you cannot expect for someone else to fix mistakes from the past. You are also at fault for holding your truth and pretending to be okay with your relationship at the time. If you chose to not speak up during the times your partner made you feel less, you need to look into your belief system and see what past trauma is making you act this way. There is a belief in you that is holding you back from fully expressing your pains and discomforts, and you have healing to do. I am so sorry because I know no one likes to hear that, but my job here is to awaken you to find your ease with life. You are never going to be one with life as long as you are not fully accepting of your emotions and your presence in this world. Holding back your discomforts and pretending to be okay for the sake of keeping an identity is not your partner's fault, regardless of what they have done. This is what awakening to love is all about; you are responsible for yourself. There is no finger-pointing in the life of the awakened. You have everything going on for you already. You are deserving of love, you see your beauty, you see your worth, and you can make life happen. You need to work on letting go of the shame and the fear and show up for who you are, show up for how you feel, and show up for what you need.

When you pretend to be okay in a relationship and silence your intuition, you are resisting life. Your intuition is always speaking to you. Go back to some past failed relationships and see that your intuition had already spoken from the beginning and told you that something was not right. We are used to ignoring our intuition because our desire to fit in or not be alone seems like a stronger need. When we choose to ignore our intuition, we sacrifice our highest good, which is aligned with what is best for our spiritual growth long-term. We replace it by a short-term satisfaction of accomplishing something that validates us outside of us. And yes, you guessed it right, that is the ego winning you over one more time.

It is not surprising at all that we have chosen many times to ignore our intuition. We have been wired to follow a road map outside of us and to respond to the authority of those outside of us. We have been told since we are kids what to do. Some minds have actually stood up for themselves during their growth process and have become an authority on others. These minds live in the fake illusion that they get to control those around them, including their love partners. Other minds always kept the submissive attitude and only respond to life by being told what to do. These minds do great with a partner that tends to be more controlling. It seems like a perfect balance, but it is one of the many reasons this world is at war and not at peace. Both minds are not at ease with life. One is angry trying to control, and the other one is at pain being controlled. Both minds are seeking the same thing, freedom, which only comes through peace of mind. Our true wiring is to listen to ourselves. Your journey in this world is to realize that you have a path that is unique to you only. You know through your feelings what you should be doing right now. If you are not at peace in your relationship, if your needs are not met, if it is more healing to be alone, it is time to move on. You do not need me or anyone to help you through it. You do not need to go back and dissect your relationship and seek blame. You simply need to pull your partner into a calm conversation and communicate the simple and honest words "I am not happy."

What happens next is always a mystery. I am writing a book about changing the way we perceive life, so I do believe that people can change. Your partner making you a promise that he or she will change is not the change you need. Demanding someone to change in their actions is not the change you need either. Both of those are the same. You are again throwing a fishing line outside of your body to seek outside healing. When you demand promises and changes from your partner in order to heal your pain, you have created codependency in your relationship. An awakened second chance to your partner is your partner properly understanding your pain and becoming aware of where you hurt. Remember that love between two people is growth through healing. Healing comes from awareness. That is all you need to heal, to be fully aware of your wounds. The rest follows at its own timing... Defining the future of the relationship is control or fear. Those are not awakened solutions anymore; those are egoistic mind games. The solution is right here, right now, and all we can do right now is understand your pain and show compassion and love it, not plan for their future healing.

I know that this might seem complicated at first, but it truly is a simple concept once you grasp it. All it boils down to is that you are conflicted inside. You are not healing anymore, and your relationship is creating pain. Your mind wants to make up a story of how tomorrow will be better and how you can move on, and your soul is protecting your heart from breaking. Yes, we are terrified of heartbreak for some odd reason. It is almost like we feel bad about crying. You must remain present, though. Your second chances with your partner will only happen if he or she is aware of your needs today. Otherwise, my friend, for your highest good open the window and let the wind just blow it all away. Let it clean what is on its path, so you can keep moving on your journey of spiritual growth.

Choosing to continue a relationship, well knowing that your needs are not met, will diminish your sense of presence. It will be too painful for you to be aware that you are not happy every day of your life. If you settle and decide to pretend that you are okay, your ego will begin to take over. The ego is an expert at making you feel like a winner. A fake illusion that your partner is changing for the better will begin to happen. It is a fake illusion because your partner is really not changing. Your amazing soul once again settled for less than its own calling. Just like it happened many times in your past, your flame shuts down, and you adapt to your environment. When you adapt to your environment, it gives you the fake illusion that things are better now. Remember when you were a child, and you were told to stop playing in the water because you were going to get cold? You knew you were having fun and you were not cold, but you still had to obey and settle. You were sad for a while, but soon enough you found something to do inside the house, and it was all good. You'd still rather be outside playing in the water, but your mind found a way to adapt and make life seem right again, even though it knew there was a better way.

You might not know me personally, but I want you to know that if today you realized that it is time to move on from your partner, I am extremely proud of you. It is a very tough decision to come to, but it is also a great accomplishment for your personal growth. You have come to realize that there is no longer healing happening for you and your partner, and instead you are both creating more pain for each other. Rather than settling, you decided to take a step into the unknown and create the space again for you to heal on your own and allow for new beginnings. You took a step toward being one with life. Being with someone at this point of your life maybe felt like you were resisting your own existence, and being alone will allow you to flow with this universe. Breaking up is never easy, and it takes a lot of strength, but I commend you for taking a step forward to expressing yourself fully in this lifetime. I am proud of you because you said yes to yourself.

Whether you decided to move on or your partner did, heartbreak could still be a part of this moving-on process. Not enough is said about heartbreak because I believe no one has mastered it enough to be able to teach you how to avoid it. I choose to tell you that heartbreak is a very important part of life, and you most experience it. Your heart doesn't need to break just because of the loss of love. Your heart breaks because of disappointment. The heart breaks because we had found a good path to follow, and it led us to a dead end. Your heart breaks because you thought someone loved you, and now you realized it is gone, and now you are left with nothing because you still don't know how to love yourself. Now we must pull ourselves together again and try a new path. The beautiful thing about heart-break is that it is one of the few moments in this life that we allow faith to lead the way. When our heart breaks, we take our hands away from the wheel. We sit down and we cry. We are crying because we are disappointed. We are crying because we are tired. We are crying because we don't know what is next.

Wonderful things come out of heartbreak because we surrender our path. Remember that one of our worst ene-mies is that mindset of "I know," and it applies to love too. It doesn't matter how awake you are; a part of you holds on to your partner with this concept of "I know we are together," and it represents a sense of safety and direction for your life. So when we lose that sense of stability, our heart breaks. We cry out for loss of direction. And please cry, let your heart break and do not rush this process. Allow the heartbreak process to let your emotions out, capture the lessons and pains that are coming out. Try to stay in that moment until you feel recovered. It is wonderful to be in that surrendered stage because you allow the universe to drive for a little bit. One of my favorite love stories is from one of my dear friends, Gaby. She went through a major heartbreak. Both she and her partner decided to end a relationship because of lack of growth and unmet expectations. She already had a girls' trip planned to Europe so she went through with it. She cried on the way to the airport, waiting for the airplane, and inside the eight-hour plane ride. A random guy on the airplane came and offered consolation, and they became friends. Years later, married with two kids, this random guy who is her husband tells the story that when he saw her cry like that, he promised to himself that he would do whatever it took to make her life better. And he did. Gaby let go of the control over her love life, and the answer was closer than she ever thought. Can you imagine all the possibilities that are available for you the day you stop seeing life through your lens and manifesting with the same few characters you have been in the past?

Heartbreak is a beautiful thing; you surrender to life, and so many emotions and redirections come from it. Your heart is meant to break. No one teaches you how to avoid heartbreak because you are not supposed to. You are supposed to welcome this process and remain present and observe, observe all that's coming out from the depths of your soul. Allow anyone who wants to come out to do so and recover at your timing. My friend, you are deserving of love. You are meant to be one with life and at ease with what's happening. Please do not settle for less than healing, for less than growth. Allow yourself to fully express your-self in this lifetime. I say allow yourself because it is all in your hands. See your beauty, see your worth, and be aware that you have all that you need in this life to live the best feelings and emotions. Just believe that this is your time, the past is gone, and it doesn't hold you back anymore. Tell that child that still lives in you that it is over now, and we can go back to loving who we are.

Awakening to Happiness

Life can be so easy when we show no resistance to what is. We are one with everything that is around us, and it seems that it is only us, humans, who are fighting. We are the only ones who are miserable and the ones who never seem to get enough from life. I had planned on writing this book for so long, but I was waiting for the day I had a formula to share or a way that I could give people maybe a three-step process into awakening. Years after, I realized that there is truly nothing to teach. All I can do for you here is keep showing you how asleep we have been, and hopefully you can begin unpacking some of that unnecessary baggage we carry in our minds. It all comes down to unlearning the process we have learned to live by. All we need is an open mind to explore a new way of observing life; prioritize yourself before you can be of service to this world.

Awakening to happiness could be by far the most desired feeling by all of us every single day. Why wouldn't we want to be in a state of joy and contentment every day regardless of our circumstances? Have you ever asked someone if they are happy with their life? Usually that question is followed by a profound and confusing silence. The answer usually starts by a shaky "well…" and some sort of excuse is made up as of what the holdup is. I will admit to you right here that that is exactly how I used to respond to that question. It was never enough; I always had something that I was waiting for in order to fulfill my ability to be happy.

The sad part is that in this process of waiting for that magical moment to arrive or that major accomplishment to happen, happiness never seems to arrive. The result is that we forget how to be happy. Most people in this world have no clue what happiness is. Happiness is being able to be in a place of joy and contentment with your present moment, regardless of the circumstances. The key here is this: *regardless of the circumstances*. That is the part that they forgot to teach you about happiness. Life is always happening; challenges are always developing. Happiness is a state of mind that will allow you to face your normal life but with a sense of freedom and joy. Challenges will never go away.

We forgot how to be happy because instead we were taught to idolize a life that doesn't exist. You started creating this huge checklist of items you needed in your life before you could be happy. You needed to be fit, rich, famous, married, have kids, be successful, and drive that car and own that house, etc. And to top it all off, you hoped that your state of mind was great so you could enjoy it all and finally be happy. Instead, you are living a life that maybe when you are at the top of your fitness you are going through a divorce, or when you finally get married you find out that someone you love is about to pass away. And guess what, my friend? That's more like it. The illusion that life is a smooth sail is just that—an illusion. Life is always happening because it is not just your life. It is the entire world influencing our environment. The economy is changing, the climate is changing, politics are changing, the school system is changing, and your life is part of this whole. Some days will be easier than others, but all days will be part of this rapidly changing world.

Once again, you are probably expecting me to ask you to settle for less of what you want. Again, I promise I am not; what I am going to do is just like before—show you a way that you might have been ignoring all the way along. Happiness only exists when there is freedom, and freedom to your life can only happen when you are carrying less with you. Happiness is about letting go of the burden we keep putting on us. Awakening to happiness is realizing that you do not have to wait for it anymore. Happiness is actually right here and right now; you just cannot feel it yet. Why? Because you are searching for it. Your mind is trained to search for happiness and not be in happiness. If you are searching for something, you accept that is not here. And if you have agreed to the fact that happiness is not here now, guess what you have also agreed to that is actually here instead? Pain, unhappiness, and suffering. We have to end the search somehow; we must realize that we are looking in the wrong places, and there's one place we don't look often. Right here, right now.

I do not want you to beat yourself up and make you think that you have been wrong all this time. This journey is not about proving you wrong. This journey we are taking together is about awakening and realizing what we have been missing. We prioritize the wrong things in our lives. Your inner world is your number-one priority, and every-thing outside of you just comes second. Just like peace and love, happiness operates from a place of acceptance and being one with life. Accepting events for what they are. Happiness is not about settling; it is about not depending anymore on the world to determine its presence in your life. Awakening to happiness will make you realize that all the power you were hoping for in the past is now available for you right here and right now. When you find the happiness in the now, all your actions will be more powerful than before, and you will finally be able to create a life that is meaningful to you. I always like to say this: nothing positive can ever come out of an unhappy mind, and on the contrary all positive things come from a happy mind. I'm excited to see all the good that will start pouring from you once you awaken to see the happiness around you.

A Test of Faith

Life is a test of faith. Every day, no matter your path, you will be faced with obstacles. Obstacles will always challenge not only your ability to resolve them but also your ability to stay awake and see beyond them. Awakening to happiness is realizing that every obstacle you face in your daily life can be used as a stepping stone into the ultimate person you wish to become. When we are living life unconsciously or asleep, we see obstacles as roadblocks between ourselves and who we wish to become. We do not see the opportunity for spiritual growth that each one of them presents. When we see obstacles as roadblocks, our minds have no choices but to divide. The thoughts you have in your mind about expecting life leading you to a better self do not match the fearful energy in your body facing the obstacles. You have one side of you pushing you to believe that everything will be fine, and another side telling you that nothing is right in this moment. A great amount of turbulence happens inside of you, which creates anger and fear. The body can only be at this state for a certain amount of time before it breaks. Most people revert back to losing faith and falling back asleep into fearful thoughts. This is where collective thinking is born. Our minds do not want to be stressed feeling something that the rest of the world doesn't feel. It's easier to just shut down and just collectively feel what the people around us are feeling. Sharing a vision and a feeling gives us safety, but it also shuts down faith.

Faith is simply knowing that everything is happening for a bigger reason. Faith is what gives us the resilience to overcome obstacles, knowing that all events are part of the process. Faith is presence, and it only happens in the now. You can only have faith when you are awake and in the moment. You simply look at your circumstances and understand that experiencing human form is about growth, and growth only happens when we are faced with challenges that force us to choose faith over fear. The only way you choose faith over fear is when you shake hands with the present. Remember that being awake is being at ease with life. Think of all the examples of nature from before; animals in nature face challenges every single day just like you and me. But they don't stress about it; they just jump into action and detach from the results. You do not have to be thrilled about what is happening right now, but you have to accept it for what it is. You have to know by now that you have overcome 100 percent of your obstacles up to this day, and this will be another day to get you closer to your higher self. It doesn't matter if you are Catholic, Buddhist,

Muslim, Jewish, or if you do not believe in anything. The big picture comes down to "Do you believe in your journey?" If you do not believe in your journey, you are part of the collective thinking. You might say that you do, but deep inside you have no idea where life is taking you, and you just keep reacting to the changes that life throws at you.

When turtles are born, they find the light of the stars reflecting on the ocean. That is their guide to find the water for the first time. They come out of the shell at night and just follow the light into the water. Recent studies have shown that the lights of cities and buildings by the beach confuse the turtles, and the turtles turn in the opposite direction of the water. This is what collective thinking is doing to your life. Faith is the light from the stars that is always shining and guiding you to your highest good. Your job is to believe in your journey and follow your light. The collective thinking is shining lights at you from everywhere. You react and keep following everyone into the wrong path, well knowing that you should trust your instinct. All it takes is for you to watch the news for a couple weeks straight, and you will see how reactive to life you've become. The news makes you so fearful and aggressive toward the world. All it takes is for a more important event to take place, and then all the stuff they had you worried about doesn't matter anymore. Now you are all worked up over something else.

Today, I want you to awake into happiness, and one of the biggest pieces to be able to accomplish this is for you to realize that life is a test of faith. Earlier in the book I walked you through manifesting things into your life, we talked about life's purpose, and we talked about being deserving of love. All those concepts are strong and necessary for you to remain awake in this journey. But when you get all of those things that you are aiming for, I want you to be happy. I want you to be able to enjoy them. See, the issue is that for as long as you are alive, you still have growth to do, and challenges will keep presenting themselves. You are a diamond in this world, and you will be under pressure until you are the perfect gem. The day you are the perfect gem, your mission is accomplished, and you will more than likely perish out of your physical form. But this process can be fun; happiness can be with you all day, every day. But you have to tune into it. You have to set your station to the right channel and start seeing your life through lens of faith.

Faith comes down to this: "No matter what happens to me, I choose to believe that everything happening today will turn out better than I ever even imagined." Read that again. Maybe it sounds a little weird saying it the first time. Read it over and over and over again until is part of your belief. I read it every morning. What I love about that affirmation is that it reminds me to not be attached—not be attached to the money I make or the results I want. To not waste too much time thinking if I have what it takes to solve this problem I am faced with today or not. It reminds me to not stress too much about having answers or not. It reminds me to put my faith above all circumstances and results and simply be able to say that, no matter what happens, it is always working in my favor. It makes you surrender your control, and with humbleness you turn to the universe and say, "I know what I want, but I do not know all the ways possible to get there, so I will accept this challenges today, knowing you are a leading me in the right direction."

The asleep mind reacts to an affirmation like that with comments like "Oh that's just silly." The egoistic mind knows all the answers and the only few ways to get to your goals. The egoistic mind thinks that happiness is the light at the end of the tunnel. It believes that happiness is not here today because of obstacles. It believes that obstacles make life harder and lead nowhere. The egoistic mind suffers more and has higher chances of never manifesting good into our lives. The moment that the obstacles are too painful, the ego just wants you to give up. Most of this world is asleep, and that's why most people settle. They settle for a job they dislike because doing what they love has many obstacles; they settle for unhappiness because moving on is too uncertain. But all of that can be woken up by having faith, by believing that no matter what, you will always be okay and taking the leap into happiness. The only way you will live happy is when faith is part of your daily life. Through faith, you will always be able to look through the challenges of the daily grind.

You will find especially that, after reading a book like this, you might get inspired to want to create more of what you want in your life. This is certainly my goal, to free you from the stories that society has put in your head and empower you to create a journey that you enjoy living. A lot of this new way of thinking happens in your conscious mind. What I mean is that you will have to take the time daily to say your affirmations, to practice self-love, to check in with your thinking, and to kick your ego out of your present. Those are also important and necessary steps, but there is a silent demon that lives within you and me. Your unconscious mind is loaded with the negative thinking from the past. All those years asleep, being told what to do, getting told you couldn't do it, and listening to endless talks about you not having enough money, not having enough resources, and not having enough education. All of that is deep down in your unconscious mind, and unfortunately that's where your beliefs come from. So you can say one thousand times as loud as you can, "I deserve love," but if the belief way in there is "I am not good enough," then the ladder will be winner.

It's really discouraging because finally you wake up and become aware of your power to create the life you desire, and now you become your biggest sabotage. The negative thoughts do not come up clearly. So for example, for someone that doesn't think they are not good enough, it won't show up as a thought that says, "I am not good enough," but it shows up more like a feeling. So say what you want to feel clearly. "Love comes to me easily." Now pay attention to how you feel inside. Are you excited and happy listening to this? If you are, then great, and probably chances are that you are not hurting for love either right now. If you feel uncomfortable or negative about it, then there is your demon belief that we need to get rid of. Also, chances are that you are stressed about love right there. Simple how we can prove fairly quickly how we live in the circumstances of our belief system. See, the things that you lack right now are the ones you have the hardest time manifesting. At the same time, the areas you are struggling to master in your life are probably the same ones you have some wicked belief system within you that we have to clean out.

Attacking each one of these negative beliefs could be a very long process. I'm not saying it is impossible, but it will for sure take a while to accomplish. My technique is a little easier than that. The way to change the belief is to pay attention to your internal environment throughout the day. Why are you so angry? Why are you depressed today? Why are you feeling down? What are you scared about? Think about those questions. If I am telling you right now that you live in the circumstances of your thoughts, if I am telling you all the ways you can be empowered and awakened into being at peace, into manifesting what you want, into being in love, then why are you still in pain? The real answer is because you still don't believe me. It is that simple. As thrilled as you might be and as many aha moments you might have had throughout this book, you are not happy because you still think that this is not possible for you. You might think you are angry, sad, or depressed because the things you want are not here yet. But that is another lie of the ego. If I give you an airplane ticket for your Hawaii vacation, you are excited for this vacation whether it is tomorrow or in three months. You believe it, you can hold the ticket, and you can see it. What I am asking you to do in this book, you cannot see it, you cannot touch it. This is all just messing with your thoughts and beliefs. Once again, your mind is turned outward. The confirmations come from outside of you; they have never come from within. It is the car that made you happy, the house, the grade, the wedding party, and the looks of your partner. We do not know how to seek for confirmations inside. We do not know how to have faith, and therefore we have no clue how to awaken into happiness.

Here is how we are going to change this: I am not going to make you go down searching for every single one of your negative beliefs. You can, and I encourage you to do that through your life journey. But those events bring out pain, and it's better to be done with a coach or therapist to help you through searching and analyzing your thinking. Instead, I want you to have bigger thoughts just like the one from before. "What if everything turns out better than I ever even imagined it could?" "Reminder: why am I upset when I know that there is so much more coming my way?" "Why am I suffering when I know that nothing outside of me has power over me?" "This is just part of the process. I am certain it will lead to a better day."

Have optimism over your negativity. We all have a negative mind, and I have never experienced it going away completely. What I have experienced is myself becoming aware of my thinking. And as soon as I see my mind wanting to go down the spiral staircase, I dismiss it. I say things like "Oh well, if that becomes a problem, I am sure I'll figure it out like everything else." "I know where I'm headed in my life, and I am sure that this is another step in the process." Be aware of your brain and when you feel negativity; do not let it get out of hand. Training your brain is like training your pet. You have to repeat, repeat, repeat, and it just starts to stick slowly. Bottom line is, have thoughts that are bigger than your day-to-day hustle. Yes, life might suck for you today, but you know your success is not in question. And that is having faith in your journey. When every obstacle is never big enough to question your destination.

Life is a test of faith. Challenges will always come your way. Do you believe that you are deserving of the things you want in your life? Are you worthy of your dreams? Do you want to be awakened into seeing happiness every day in your life? Then have faith, my friend. Have faith in yourself, and have faith in your life. If you keep questioning your destination and breaking down every obstacle, all you keep putting out there is you still don't believe you are deserving of the things you want. No one can help you but you, and it is as simple as starting where you are, simply believing that no matter what the storm is looking like, you always have a favorable wind. I believe in you, and I think you should start being happy about all that's coming your way. More importantly, learn to embrace all the good that is here today; remember that the grace of God was a promise for today, not tomorrow.

Attachments

One of the most important pieces to be awakened into happiness is letting go of the expectations in your mind. Not an easy task to accomplish when we live in a society that is always asking us to plan for tomorrow. Some of my favorite advertisements on TV are the ones for the companies that are trying to get you to buy a policy to cover the cost of your funeral service and burial. Like, really? I mean I get it: it's all about relieving the family from burden, but still, we are already at that point where people plan what to do with their remains. I would never forget years ago while visiting my grandfather's grave, I overheard a lady in the background trying to select which spot she wanted to be buried at. I was very young at the time, and I remember being so confused by it. Is it really going to make a difference for her? But those are prime examples of who we are as a society. Any bit of control that we can take of our future, we jump on it. We budget, we save, we plan, and then we wait for better days to come.

If I could eliminate one thing from our lives today, it would be the ability to wait. Waiting and attachment work incredibly good together. We have an attachment to a story, and as a result of that we wait until that story manifests itself. I strongly believe that if we did not have the ability to wait, we will be more present and see more of what is available for us right now. It sounds like I am telling you to settle for what is around you and not wait for what you really want. I am actually not asking you to settle at all. What I want you to do is expand your attention to see what is around you right now. Manifesting is aligning your present energy with the things you desire in your life, but at no point you enter in denial of your present. Waiting is a denial of the present, which as a result traps you in this mindset of never being enough. As crazy as this sounds, I guarantee that you have already met your soul mate multiple times. I guarantee that you have hundreds of ways to becoming a millionaire already, you have all you need right now to live your purpose, and you have all the time to be physically fit. What is holding you back is the waiting game. Your mind is so set on the story you have going on that you cannot seem to act with what is around. Waiting is a game of patience. Waiting takes our eyes from the present and puts them in the future. Waiting blocks you from seeing what is available to you in the present. Waiting is the unconscious mind's favorite game; it promises that tomorrow will be better, and today we can just be asleep. But in reality, there are no guarantees that the story you wait for will manifest itself; the only thing that it guarantees is less suffering. Pay attention to this: waiting for something allows you to settle for less today. If you tell yourself, "I'll wait for the right person to come into my life," today you get to settle for being alone. If you tell yourself, "I am waiting for my promotion to finally enjoy going to work today," you settle for going to a job you do not enjoy.

It all comes down to this. If you are waiting for something so your life can get better, your mind is attached to a story. This story allows you to be okay with the fact that you are not okay with your present circumstances. You might find this a little contradicting, since a couple chapters ago I was asking you to align your energy with the things that you want in your life. But this is the awakening moment everyone misses. Aligning yourself with what you want does not mean you now get to wait for it. Aligning yourself with what you want means truly feeling and believing that you are deserving of fulfilling all your desires in this lifetime. Yet if that belief and alignment is happening, it brings joy and peace to your present, and you start taking advantage of all opportunities around. This is where you become powerful. When you are able to remain in stillness in your present because you know that circumstances outside of you have no power over your energy and your alignment. Waiting is not an awake state. Waiting is denial of the present circumstances that puts you in a position of

"I need this in order to feel that." And that is the state that you continue to live. Remember that we live in the circumstances of our thoughts. If you keep living in this state of "I still don't have that," the result is "Okay, you still don't have that." And I am certain that you know this already, but I'll still mention it. There is no happiness whatsoever in that state of mind.

Happiness can only exist inside of a mind that has freed itself from the uncertainty of the future. The grace of God was only promised for today. Chances are, most will wake up tomorrow and get the opportunity to keep living, but for others today might be their last chance. No one knows the future; no one knows how anything will actually turn out. Remember, the goal is to feel at peace, to be in love, and to be happy. What else could be missing from your life if you felt this way every day? So it is time to start awakening yourself and realize what your daily habits are that keep preventing you from feeling this way. Be at peace knowing that you have all it takes to manifest whatever you want in this life; just know that you deserve it and believe. Fall in love with the uniqueness of who you are and the journey you live in. Know your worth. Finally, combine those pieces and realize that you have nothing to wait for anymore; you can start being happy. If the things you want are not here today, you know you deserve them, and you know the story will unfold. So be in the state of mind of joy and gratitude of where you are today. Here is a simple example. If you win the lottery today, and the money will not be in your bank for another two weeks, how would you feel today? Do you have the money to spend it yet? No. Are you feeling peace, happiness, and gratitude in your present circumstances because of what you know your worth is? Yes. Then that's the fine line right there between waiting and being deserving. Just like the test of faith, check in with your emotions, and make sure that you are in the right state of mind.

Awakening to happiness is detaching yourself from waiting and controlling results. You will suffer less the day that you surrender a little the control you are trying to have of the outside world. That mindset becomes much easier when you change the direction you are aiming for. Most people consume their lives with small thinking. So the perfect example is politics. If you are in a presidential-election year, you can see how people portray their political inclinations like it is a life-or-death situation. It almost becomes like the day of the elections represents the end of the world. People do anything in their power to influence others and weigh into what they believe should be the winner. Of course, only one team can win at the end. And then it's over, and we go back to regular programming. Pretty much months are spent fighting trying to control a result that seemed to define life completely, and one day it just passes, and that is it. The interesting part, though, are the people that are trying to control politics; they are doing it from their own social media influencing, or their personal friendships. They consume their entire existence, thinking that what they are doing is actually changing the results of something as massive as a presidential election. I believe that more pain and anger is created than actually influencing people who the winning candidate should be. What is even crazier about all this is that most people are not even influenced by politics. Most people have a job, and they will continue to make the same amount of money, and they will continue to pay taxes and live their life. So where I'm getting at is how many people can you think of in your life right now that have sacrificed the treasure of their time and existence to influence others on who should they be voting for? These people could have used all these energy and time to be in alignment with their own manifestation and becoming a better or stronger self. But instead they gave it all away. That is small thinking. You live in so much pain, in so much anger, and the results have minimal impact in your life. You spend so much time angry and trying to control others, well knowing that you have zero control over what others think. So why are your eggs in that basket?

It is painful to watch sometimes how much potential we have as individuals and how it all goes to waste just because we are so attached to results that mean absolutely nothing to our highest good. Changing people, telling people what to do, criticizing others, passing judgment, and gossiping. It all comes down to control. It comes down to the fact that since we have no idea of what to do with ourselves, we choose to see if we have any control over someone else.

Aim higher, my friend. Think bigger. I cannot emphasize this enough. Believe things are turning out better than you imagined. Believe life is always to your favor. And this is not some positivity PR I am throwing at you. Please look back at your life. It is only getting better; you are so much more of an aware human today than you were one, two, or ten years ago. It all comes down to wisdom, and it just keeps accumulating. So why would you think that now is any different? Life is in your favor. No need to label events as good or bad. Whether the event is pleasant or not, so pleasant they both have one thing in common—you rise. Every single time, you rise to become someone better than you were before. So from now on, when you are faced with a situation that challenges you, do your best. Do what you truly feel inside you should be doing. If you don't know, then wait for an answer. Listen to your intuition and act accordingly. Then just let it go. Your job in this universe starts with setting intentions, and it ends with your actions. The results are out of your control, so there is no point in worrying about it. Just know that it is always working in your favor, and your worth is never a question.

Awakening to happiness is finding the joy in the now, and that is only possible when you allow yourself to live right now and not have your mind consumed trying to figure how to control something it can't. If you want to understand what insanity means, just take look around. What is truly under someone's control? Their thoughts, their beliefs, and their actions. What are most people trying to control? The outcome of events, the way others think, and the collective thinking. It is pure insanity. It is almost like people do not want to take one bit of responsibility for themselves. But you know who is leading this insanity, right? It's our dear friend, the ego. The ego is saying this: "Please do not make me feel I'm wrong, so just agree with what I'm saying." "Please let me have the results I expected at the timing I wanted because I cannot face the present moment." Let go of the attachment of controlling the results; let go of your denial of your present while you wait for more.

I want you to start thinking about the bigger picture. Do not sweat the daily challenges; they pass quickly. Your internal environment is what defines everything that is ahead, so please stop reacting to small things. Stop reacting to what people say or do. Stop reacting to the person that does not agree with what you say. Stop getting devastated because your results don't match what you have in mind, and just keep your eyes on the big picture. The people that have accomplished great things in this world waste little time sweating the small stuff or grieving their failures. They fail and have battles just like you and me. But they never take their eyes away from the bigger picture. Let go of your attachment to what you know.

If you want to awaken to happiness, you have to start entering this world with almost like a sense of curiosity. A playful, childlike energy. You keep your eyes on your target, and you begin your day open to miracles. What are miracles? Unexpected events that surprise you into results you never imagined possible. How can you receive a miracle if you are not open to them? You have to let go of what you know. Stop talking so much and listen. Listen to all sides of the story, and make up your own. Stop surrounding yourself so much with people that idolize you, and be open to the people that challenge you a bit. And just be quiet and listen. Hear what others have to say about you. Just like the journey of being in love. Let people hold the mirror up a little bit, and try to stay quiet—do not get defensive. Just say thank you. Be powerful enough to listen to perspective and not take it personal. Be brave enough to dissect what the world is saying and come up with your opinion. And when you come up with an opinion, still don't take it too seriously. I love this quote: "The challenge is understanding something enough to think you are right but not enough to know you are wrong."

That is for sure your challenge in this life. Without ruining your self-worth, start to think you are wrong more often. And start listening. Here is what it comes down to, my friend. You are meant to live at peace, you are meant to be happy, and you are meant to feel in love. If you do not feel that right now, you are wrong. And we have to search, and we have to see what we are perceiving. I know I don't feel that way every minute of the day, and I am in the same journey as you. Anytime I catch my feelings hurt or reacting over something, I am no longer peaceful, in love, or happy so I have fallen off my vibration. I need to do work inside and align myself. Think big thoughts that help me see beyond my ego. "Life is always on my favor." "This is all temporary and it will pass." "What if all this turns out better than I ever imagined?" "I am doing what I can and that is enough."

Happiness is a wonderful feeling, and it only exists when there is nothing to disturb it. You have probably heard this before: happiness is not a destination. This is what people meant all along when that quote was said. Happiness is here right now. What no one had told you before is that it is only here when presence is all it is. Let go of your agenda, your expectations, and your attachments to results; and know that if you know you are worth it, just smile at what today has to offer. There is nothing to worry about in regards to tomorrow; the job is done accepting what is today.

The Way People See You

Awakening to happiness involves detaching yourself from an activity that consumes the mind of those who are asleep. That activity involves attempting to control the perception of others. It has become so important for humans to have the approval of the world, that countless of hours of the day are spent trying to shift how people see us. This game is another one that is complete insanity—we will never be able to control how someone else thinks. At the same time, it is totally understandable how we got to this point. It all comes back to childhood and our mental wiring being taught that everything we need comes from outside of us. This belief gave birth to the ego, and we started competing with the world. It became important to us to understand how the world sees us, so we could get more of the things we wanted. If I act this way, maybe this group of people will want me as a friend. If I pretend to be this other way, I might find someone that wants to date me. These are all games of the egoistic mind. You have created a story, and in that story you actually made up how people are responding to you. What you have been missing all this time is to realize that everyone is playing the same game as you are. You are not more or less than the person listening to you. This is why human interaction is so unpredictable. We all have an agenda in mind, and we are aiming for a desired result.

You can only be awakened to happiness when you can just be you. Anytime that you are pretending to be someone else, in order to control the reaction that people might have toward you, you end your alignment with your higher self. You are doing things with a motive and not acting from a space of peace or love. Our soul is always craving that feeling of love and peace in order to be in a state of stillness and happiness. Your soul can only do that when it is allowed to express itself and be one with life. Once you are pretending to be something, and your fulfillment depends on the outside, you are acting from a space of fear. One of the most common examples I can think of is looking at the crowd at a concert. If you watch the crowd, you will find a few people who are present in the moment enjoying a song or dancing. These people are in the moment; they are one with life. They came to the concert to enjoy the music they want to enjoy. They are receiving the music and projecting the response that the present requires. Then you see another portion of the room with people who have their phones out, and they are more concerned about capturing the moment for social media. They have sacrificed the reason that brought them to the concert for the need to get the validation from the world of where they are. They are receiving what life is throwing at them, but their response is not present. Their response is attached to the value others will give to it in the future. Which of these concertgoers do you think is going to be more at peace at the end of the day? Obviously, the ones that let happiness depend upon themselves and not anyone else.

Throughout this book, you have seen me mention many times the egoistic mind. I waited until this chapter to talk about it because it is here where it will make the most sense. The ego is born the moment that you have an agenda outside of your physical body. The ego is the personality in you that takes over in events, and it is attempting to manipulate the world outside. The ego fogs the world from seeing who you truly are and uses words, actions, and emotions to obtain reactions from people outside. The ego is always looking to win at something. It doesn't matter whether it is something good or something sad; if the ego obtains control over someone's way of thinking, the ego is winning. The ego doesn't like to be wrong, so it acts out of fear and anger in order to manipulate another person's beliefs. At times when the ego has brainwashed the person enough, it could go to the extent of causing violence and events of mass destruction in order to get the world to see their pain.

Most of the time, the ego is covering up pain. It was too painful to be us, so it felt better to be asleep. We took over different personalities because our soul was broken, and we couldn't get what we needed from the world for just being us. See, if we would have been taught from the beginning that none of what we search for resides outside of us, we would have no choice but to look inward and live our truth. Society forced us into two different lives. We have our internal broken world that we can live in privacy, and then we have the mask we have to put on for work, in order to get that promotion and power over our coworkers. We have another mask to show on social media, so unknown followers, high school friends from back home, and people that know us see how good we are doing. Then we need another mask for our social world and love life. It is a lot to keep up with, and this is why it is no accident that people need medications at times to cope with the stress and anxiety of life. It is stressful and anxious when you are constantly having to pretend to be okay, to constantly be at competition with the world, when you are in a game of survival.

You will eventually break; you will not be able to hold it all together. For some it is a divorce that alleviates things, for others it's changing jobs and starting fresh somewhere else, and for others it is taking a social media break and separating from their friends. I started to pick up how unhappy I was when I actually needed to be alone in my house for hours and not answering the phone. I just couldn't pretend anymore when all I wanted was to cry. People will compliment me for what I did, which means my ego was a happy camper. But at the end of the day I was so unhappy, I couldn't even see it or feel it. Yes, I was good at certain things, but what does being good in the outside mean when you are totally broken inside?

Read this carefully: you are what you feel, think, and do when no one else is watching you. Have an honest look at your life behind closed doors, and just observe. With no judgment, no agenda, just observe who you are. If you are similar to me, you are going to find that maybe you can just collapse on your couch and scroll through your phone or watch TV, addicted. I remember that I became aware of the problem when I started having days off with nothing to do, and instead of using my time for useful projects and goals, I just sat there and did a whole lot of nothing. Normally, the ego comes in and tells you that you are tired, and you should take your time off and relax, which it is totally okay. There is another side to that story, though. You have retrained your mind and your life to be efficient and productive when you are in front of others. Almost like putting up a show. During that painful time of putting on a show, you tell yourself that someday when you have time you will read books and do more of the things that make you happy and maybe lose a couple pounds, etc. The truth is that none of that is true when you see how you act behind closed doors. I remember I could just lie down and stare at the ceiling for hours or call people to gossip, or even needed to get out of the house. The ego consumes our lives, and it finally gets its way. When you don't have a mask to wear in front of someone, you do not know how to be anymore. You are completely asleep. That's when you realize it is time to face the truth and explore really what is inside.

This is your awakening into happiness, when you see there is no happiness in your life. Something has to be missing. I'll tell you what that is. The relationship with yourself. The full expression of who you are and what you want to be doing, and what you want to be feeling. Yes, deep inside you want to read a book and do some workouts and explore your hobbies. But you need to almost like retrain your mind to go for it. You have to find the joy behind doing things for you and not for society. As simple as this sounds, it is such a huge step. If you have social media, go look; I think I have done it myself many times too. You start reading the book and you post the cover of the book on your Instagram story, you go working out and you need a picture online of the process, and you start your hobby and you text the group chat for you to hear what they have to say. Your ego is grasping for dear life. I am not saying it's bad for you to reveal your activities and celebrate them. But ask yourself honestly why. Why do you keep putting yourself out there? Is it because you want people to see it, or because you needed the validation? Do you feel like doing activities on your own are only fun when others validate them? Maybe you do not enjoy being with you. Maybe that's your big red flag that the relationship you have with yourself is not as relevant in your life as the relationship you have with the world.

It is a big transition, and most people do not get to that realization. But enough is enough. Please open your eyes and realize that everyone else is doing the same as you. No one cares…trust me. They pretend they do, they will comment and "heart" it, and text you back. But deep inside no one cares. You do not need to take my word for it. Just see other people's life through your life. Do you care that Molly went to the gym today? Do you care that I decided to learn how to bake bread today? You might find it's cute, but your mind is consumed by your own agenda. You have your day ahead of you and stuff you need to accomplish. You are trying to make a statement in life yourself. That's how we are. We are self-centered people when we are asleep, and we are all trying our best. It doesn't matter if we do things with the best intention. Maybe today you decided to bake bread for your entire office. Guess what? Most people loved it, and you are awesome. But you only did it because it validates you. Maybe tomorrow you decided that your boyfriend is not treating you right, so you turned off your phone and spent the day working out at the gym. Guess what? He got the point, and I am sure he knows something is up. But you did it for you; it validates you.

The ego is meshed on everything in your life. It's like a pest that when you think you kicked it out of somewhere, it starts growing somewhere else. So you probably wonder, then how? How do we end this? If I tell you how, I will be giving you another mask to wear. Now you become the ego buster, and that's another way to validate yourself. Just be, my friend. Be you. You are awesome. You have a purpose in this world. This is what I've told you this entire book. Drop your agenda. Drop your ladder. Drop the "If I do this, it leads me to that." This is the life of the awakened, the life of the birds. The life of the trees, the monkeys, the cats, and the dogs. They don't label, they do. They don't try, they are. Face your present for what is present. And more importantly, above all things, tune yourself once and for all into the abundance of this world. There is enough for everyone: enough love, enough money, enough friends, enough jobs, and enough opportunities. So just let the ego go away once and for all, and practice existing for your calling inside. A real life, a life of truth and happiness, only comes when you are real, when you show up for your truth.

I think if you are taking anything from this book, it's that you have to live this life like you are Play-Doh. If you ever got the chance to use Play-Doh, remember the texture? It sticks a little bit, but it comes off easy. Play-Doh can be turned into shapes, but it doesn't harden up so you can mold it again. That's what being awakened is, my friend. Invest in yourself; live your life. Have your identities, but stay away from the suffering. Don't let anything define you; don't waste time controlling. Don't get too caught up and be okay moving on. Understand that your journey is always bigger than your current circumstances. Remember the world of polarities we live in. No good or bad events, no good or bad people, no one is better or worse, and no one has it easier. All those labels are suffering. Those are the labels we created to cover our pains. We needed those labels in order to make ourselves feel better for what we lacked. But ask yourself this. You lacked what? Go on with your list. Oh, you lacked money, popularity, social status, education, family, and love? Okay, great… Compared to whom? And once again, here is your answer! You went outside to look. Your ego showed up again to create suffering and to tell you that someone else has it better, rather than you embracing that your journey is unique, period. Stop falling into the trap of believing that you control what people think. You waste time believing that you can control people's perceptions of you, and the way you believe people perceive you is also a story you made up in your head. You can believe all you want that they like you, but you'll never know if that's true. You can believe all you want that a person has bad feelings for you, but you will never know the truth. So the easiest thing to do is to focus on you and let it go. Awakening to happiness is very simple. Live your life. Act out of love. Find peace with your journey.

You Are Worth It

Letting go of stories and patterns in your life is key to creating the room for you to be present. Being present is the only thing that gives us access to help us feel the happiness we long for. If our minds are wrapped up in another time that is not right here and now, we are living in an illusion. That illusion can only create feelings of desire or fear that, as a result, create a mindset of denial to where we are at. We deny our present thinking about how different tomorrow may be or how different yesterday used to be. Awakening to happiness is letting go of all that story and just coming back to where you are. Come back to the presence you have in the room you are in, and just observe yourself. Start with simple things like focusing on your breath, your body, your accomplishments, the shelter you are sitting in, the clothing you are wearing, and finding gratitude. Gratitude makes us present; we come back into a space of acknowledgement of who we are.

Happiness is directly equivalent to gratitude. I want you to pay close attention to this: life will pass you by if you don't practice gratitude. And most people think they are grateful. Oh of course I am grateful for my house, but. I can see the progress in my health, but. I am grateful for the money I made this year, but. That *but*, my friend, takes the power out of the entire process of gratitude. You will always see happiness as a destination if you do not teach your mind how to take a pit stop every single day to practice gratitude. Stop thinking that one day you are going to wake up and that life will be full of rainbows, and everyone is going to be perfect and you are going to scream, "My life is perfect!" Get real. Life is about growth, and in order for you to grow, life will always be challenging you one way or another. Life can only get easier, though, if you let it. You can make it easier by starting to find the silver lining hidden in every challenge and not fall asleep in chaos on a daily basis. Part of making life easier and happy every day is the practice of gratitude. All that gratitude can be is acknowledgment. I see you and I love you. Those are powerful words to say to people and things in your life.

Say it to your home, say it to your college degree, say it to your job, say it to the food in your fridge, and say it to the money in your bank. Acknowledge it. Stop adding the *but* after because that is simply reminding yourself that your story is unfulfilled. We know, we know. Trust me, we know that you are aiming for more. We are all part of the same life, and we have all climbed the mountain just to find that there is another mountain right behind it. But you will have the power to keep climbing. If you can, stop, breathe, and look down and see how far you made it and feel the pride inside. Feel relief; feel love for your journey. In that feeling of gratitude is happiness. In that feeling of happiness, your worth continues to grow.

It doesn't matter who you are, what your race is, or what your religious views are—you are a human being, and you are worth it. You were brought into this beautiful journey called life, and you are exactly where you need to be right now. You might feel like you are a little behind of where you wish you were, or you might feel like you have lived some experiences a little too soon. That is just your mind looking outside of your soul and comparing yourself to others. This why it might feel uncomfortable, and this why we question our worth so often. When you stop looking outside, you start seeing your journey for what it is and realize that you are where you need to be. Whether you are living completely unconscious or you are awakened, life will always be poking at you. Every day will bring new events that will have you question who you really are. New parts of you will arise, and you will get to know more about who you are and the unique talents that you bring to this world. Don't stress about missing the awakening of life; it will happen. Life gets uncomfortable, and you have no choice but start to explore who you really.

This process can be painful, and it doesn't have to be. In the awakening process, a lot of moments of shame will arise. You will see parts of you that make you feel ugly. You will understand some of your actions and realize how selfish we have been. You will see how much time and effort was wasted fighting battles that only existed inside your head. This process can take away your joy and happiness, and it doesn't have to be that way. Stay present, stay strong, and power through the growth. You are worth it, and you did not know any better back then. Remember something: all of these feelings are yours and no one else's. You must create the space in you where you realize that you don't need to explain yourself anymore. You were doing what you could with what you knew. You understand now that your worth is 100 percent your responsibility. Feeling your worth based on the opinions of the world will always leave you feeling incomplete. Some people will find you amazing, while others will disagree with who you are. Awakening to happiness is cultivating your worth on your own, standing your ground with you head up, and knowing that you believe in who you are.

Self-worth is such an important tool in your life because it is the one thing that will make this awakening process stick. Self-worth is like the shell of an egg; it holds all of you together, and it protects it from the outside. You could find that some of the teaching of this book can make you very powerful very quickly. You could be ready to align yourself to something huge and make it happen. I know people that took small leaps in business aligned with purpose, and they just blew up. Here is what happens next, though: all that success can quickly become temporary if you let yourself fall back asleep. Your ego might be under control during the creation process, but once you make it to places you always wanted to be without enough self-worth, you will go back to the game of the ego. You fall back into pleasing others and living for the outside validation. The perfect example for this is the people that get rich quickly. Normally they are back to being poor within a certain period of time. They were able to manifest financial success, through proper alignment, but their lack of self-worth made them use that money to obtain all the material things they needed to make themselves feel worthy.

The way you see money will always be the biggest giveaway of how worthy you think you are. I personally did not grow up rich. I saw both of my parents work very hard and fail many times. So if anything, I grew up with the belief that money did not come very easy. The result of that is I have had to clean up my debt multiple times because anytime I could, I went to spend on stuff I couldn't afford. I believed since I was a child that having fancy things was a sign of doing okay. I went to a very privileged school, and I was always surrounded by many kids that had it all. You grow up thinking you need to have all of the things they did in order to be happy. I have resolved so many of my self-worth issues by cleaning my relationship with money. I can see that all the things that I have wanted that I found a way to purchase only gave me temporary happiness. The ego was fed for a couple days, but it got hungry again. Self-worth is about the things that you possess that no one can buy and no one can take. Your wisdom, your strengths, your knowledge, your self-love, and your beliefs. Self-worth is also how you handle your failures, the things you are still working on, and also how you see your weaknesses.

Awakening to happiness is finding peace in the fact that you won't be great at everything. There are things in life that you are going to have to consciously flip and start finding the positive out of, something that you have felt bad about. Guess what? I am five feet nine inches tall. Will I love being six two? of course I would, but can I do something about that? No, I cannot. So might as well start shaking hands with my height. I am also not that great at building things. It doesn't matter how many times I read the instruction manual; when it comes to putting stuff together, for some reason my build-it-yourself project, does not turn out so steady. It's fine; maybe it's a weakness of mine, and I own it. I laugh about it. I take the importance away from it. It doesn't make me any less of a person, and I am sure there is someone out there who would love to put together some things for my home. Remember my story from earlier about sports? That hasn't changed one bit. I think my most recent attempt to throw a ball of paper into a distant trash bin was a disaster. I am not great at sports; it's okay. I will not beat myself for that anymore. I already went to the child in my past and told him, "You are fine, don't stress anymore." In adult life sports do not matter so much. Owning your weaknesses is one of the most transforming pieces to your self-worth. Stand tall and be able to say the things you are great at and the things you need help with. No one is perfect, and no one will ever be perfect. That's why we live in a world of balance. What you lack, maybe I can help you with, and I am certain that you can help me out in some way as well.

Joel Osteen says, "What follows 'I Am' is what we are inviting into our lives." I urge you to start taking this message seriously. We are living in times where people love finding humor in demeaning themselves. And trust me, I get it—it can be funny and humorous. I have found some great laughs out of calling myself fat, lazy, immigrant. I know there is a context for all of that. But please realize that if you verbalize it, it has an origin within you. It is not just a joke. I am not trying to make you a fragile person that takes everything personal. I am simply urging you to pay attention to those "jokes" and funny references about who you are. There is a place in you that believes this to be true, and that means your self-worth is on the line. Do your daily affirmations. I understand that at times you may find that it's silly or that it feels awkward. But the reason it feels awkward is because your mind is resisting what you are saying. What you are verbalizing is not in line with what you believe is true inside of you. That is a huge red flag. Why is it awkward to say "I am beautiful," "I am worth it," "I am awesome," or "I am successful"? What is so awkward about it? If you were having trouble identifying your negative beliefs, well, there you have it. You just identified a lot that needs to be worked on. It should never feel awkward for you to speak the truth.

This entire book has been leading you over and over to the same realization. That world you see out there, that you have been attempting to understand and control, is nothing but a mirror reflecting what is in your life. It's taken me years to understand this concept because I never truly could grasp how a reflection of me could create so much suffering. So many love affairs left me feeling empty inside. So many jobs that I put so much effort into that never paid me enough. So many hours at the gym that never left me feeling good-looking enough. So many new hairstyles, outfits, and cars that still never allowed me to fit in. It all woke me up to the realization that I must be doing something wrong. I have to be missing something. And one day I looked inside and realized that the problem and the solution had been sitting in me for all these years. I had no self-worth. I realized I did not love myself. I did not find myself attractive enough; I did not think I was worth that much money. I realized I didn't think I was good enough to fit in. One day I woke up, and I felt so overwhelmed on how I would fix this entire mess. It felt easier for me to shut back down and keep settling for my daily adventures. But how can you settle for less than what you want to feel? I want peace, I want love, I want happiness, and I am deserving of it like you are. We are worth it. And that is all it takes. This is the beginning of the best days of your life. You are worth it, my friend. You are worthy of love, you are worthy of living your purpose, and you are worthy of the freedom that comes along with being your number-one fan. So please wake up and take some responsibility. Take ownership of your life once and for all. Grab a piece of paper and plan your day tomorrow, prioritize yourself, and prioritize what you need to be doing. Make the time every day to do affirmations in front of the mirror, to start spending time with your hobbies, to start working out, or to start eating right. No one can do your self-worth job. You have to look at life and take care of yourself. You have to prioritize yourself first because only when you take care of yourself first will you be able to take care of everyone around you. Stop trying to understand so much of the world around you, and start understanding who you are. Look outside at nature every day, and try to learn something from it. The world you want to experience outside, you must feel it inside you first. Peace, love, and happiness are all we long for in this life. The best part is that it already lives within you and me. You are worthy of it, so now cut ties with the outside world, set yourself free, and rekindle the love with the most important person in your life. Yourself. Promise me you will never forget that again. I need your light, we need your light, and the world needs your light.

About the Author

Born in Venezuela, Alfredo Brandt was the recipient of an academic scholarship that allowed him to migrate to the United States in 2005 to pursue a bachelor's degree in business management. After graduation he became an accountant for a corporation, but it didn't take long for Alfredo to realize that the life he was living was not feeling the way he had hoped for. This was the beginning of Alfredo's personal-growth journey, as it made him passionate to understand how he end up working a job he disliked and living a life completely distant from his true calling. In 2012, Alfredo ventured to open a fitness studio in Las Vegas, where he started to share his work of helping others through mind-body practices. Until this day he continues to work in the fitness industry, and he continues to grow in the personal-growth field through life coaching and empowering others via social media platforms. Alfredo is committed to keep creating space for humanity to wake up, take responsibility, and settle for nothing less than their true calling in life.

CPSIA information can be obtained
at www.ICGtesting.com
Printed in the USA
BVHW070456010621
608480BV00001B/28